MOUNTAIN BIKE GUIDE

North Wales

by

Pete Bursnall

ERNEST

Published by The Ernest Press 1995
© Copyright Pete Bursnall

ISBN 0 948153 18 0

British Library Cataloguing-in-Publication Data has been registered
with the British Library in Wetherby and is available on request.

Typeset by Askvik Språktjenester A/S, Norway
Printed by St Edmundsbury Press
Sketch-maps by Gary Tompsett
Front cover illustration: Nigel Shepherd
Rear cover illustration: Nigel Shepherd

Disclaimer:
**Whilst we have made every effort to achieve accuracy in the
production of material for use in this guide book, the author,
publishers and copyright owners can take no responsibility
for: trespass, irresponsible riding, any loss or damage to
persons or property suffered as a result of the route
descriptions or advice offered in this book.**

**The inclusion of a route in this guide does not guarantee
that the path/track will remain a right of way; if conflict with
landowners occurs, please be polite and leave by the shortest
available route, then check the situation with the relevant
authority.**

**It is worthwhile, as a footnote to this disclaimer, to emphasise
that riders should give way to both pedestrians and horse riders,
and should make every effort to warn others of their presence.**

The following are extracts from the leaflet produced by the Snowdonia National Park in 1995, "National Voluntary Cycling Agreement Snowdonia".

NATIONAL VOLUNTARY CYCLING AGREEMENT SNOWDONIA

The high level of use of the bridleways to the summit of Snowdon for off-road cycling has led to serious fears about erosion and the safety of walkers.

The following voluntary agreement to remedy this problem has been negotiated between the cycling organisations, the Sports Council for Wales, Gwynedd County Council and Snowdonia National Park Authority.

10.00am to 5.00pm from 1st June - 30th September. Please do not cycle to or from the summit of Snowdon. From October to end of May - full access.

CYTUNDEB BEICIO GWIRFODDOL CENEDLAETHOL ERYRI

Mae lefel uchel defnydd beicwyr ar lwybrau march i gopa'r Wyddfa wedi creu ofnau difrifol ynghylch erydiad a diogelwch cerddwyr.

Mae'r cytundeb gwirfoddol canlynol i geisio datrys y broblem yn ganlyniad trafodaethau rhwng y cymdeithasau beicio, Cyngor Chwaraeon Cymru, Cyngor Sir Gwynedd ac Awdurdod y Parc Cenediaethol.

10.00am i 5.00pm o Fehefin 1af - Medi 30ain. Peidiwch a beicio i gopa'r Wyddfa, nac oddi yno, os gwelwch yn dda. O Hydref i ddiwedd Mai - mynediad llawn.

PLEASE SUPPORT THIS AGREEMENT
CEFNOGWCH Y CYTUNDEB HWN, OS GWELWCH YN DDA

CONTENTS

NATIONAL VOLUNTARY CYCLING AGREEMENT SNOWDONIA iii
ROUTE INDEX MAP vi
KEY TO SKETCH MAPS vii
INTRODUCTION 8
CODES OF CONDUCT 9
EQUIPMENT AND CLOTHING 10
SAFETY AND FIRST-AID 12
MAP WORK 14
COMPASS 18
FOREST AREAS 23

THE ROUTES

RUTHIN AREA

1 : LLANGOLLEN 26
2 : CLWYDIAN RANGE 32
3 : CLOCAENOG FOREST 36

BALA AREA

4 : MYNYDD MYNYLLOD 40
5 : BWLCH MAEN GWYNEDD 44
6 : LAKE VYRNWY CIRCUIT 48
7 : COED GORDDERW 54

BARMOUTH AREA

8 : MAWDDACH ESTUARY 60
9 : CIRCUIT OF CADAIR IDRIS 64
10 : BRYNCRUG CIRCUIT 70

RHINOGAU AREA

11 : TALSARNAU TO DYFFRYN 74
12 : TRAWSFYNYDD 78

ANGLESEY

13 : Beaumaris 82

CARNEDDAU AREA

14 : Cefn Côch 86
15 : Llyn Eigiau 90
16 : Llyn Cowlyd to Llyn Geirionydd 94

BETWS-Y-COED AREA

17 : Llyn Crafnant 98
18 : Llyn y Parc 102
19 : Llyn Elsi Reservoir 106

SNOWDON AREA

20 : Circuit of Moel Siabod 110
21 : Cefn Glas and Sarn Helen 116
22 : Circuit of Moel Hebog 120
23 : Beddgelert Forest 124
24 : Bwlch Cwm Llan 128
25 : Maesgwm (Telegraph Valley) 132
26 : Yr Wyddfa (Snowdon) 136

Other Rides 141

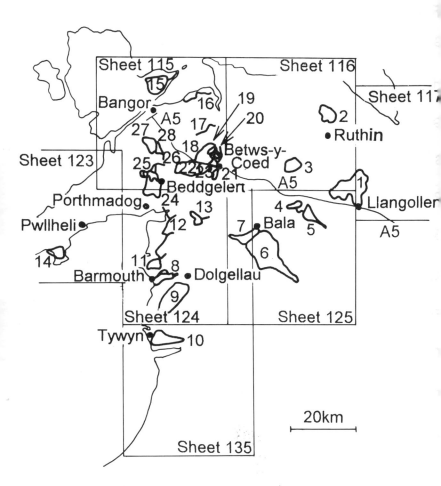

Route Index Map

Route Map Symbols

Good Downhill	☺	Caution/Danger	☠
Horrible Uphill	☹	Ford/River Crossing	⛵
Grid North Arrow	↑	Carry	
Scale	1km	View Point	◁
Railway & Station	+++o+++	On Foot Only	
Buildings	■ ■	Technical Section	
Route Direction	⟶	Difficult Navigation	?
Forest	✳ ✳	Castle/Fort	
Track	= = =	Phone	
Road	═══	A Fish	⋈○
Single Track	– – –	Dam Wall	
Stone Age Antiquities	∴∴	Radio Mast	
Footpath (No Access)	· · · · ·	Cliff	

This book is dedicated with love to Aila.

Thanks are once again due to my parents Dave and Chris for their support, encouragement and assistance in checking routes and taking photos. Thanks to all those who have ridden with me over the past months; Aila Treharne Bursnall, Andy Elder, Pete Griffiths, Tim Hakim, Dave "the leg" Hollingham, Iwan Jones, Hugh Morgan, Hugh Perkins, Clare Salmond, Rod White, Stormont, Tim, Gary 'n' Tig!

Thanks again to Douglas for his even better cartoons and, retrospectively, thanks to the Crazy Californian Dan "Woody" Woodward for starting off the whole thing in Chamonix some years ago!

Thanks to David Archer, Gareth Davies and John Ellis Roberts of the Snowdonia National Park for their assistance in checking and re-checking the contents.

Thanks are also due to Julian Salmon of the Country Landowners Association, Colin Palmer, Off-road Co-ordinator for the CTC, and Craig Williams of the Forestry Enterprise for their assistance.

Finally, many thanks to Adrian Walls of the Clwyd County Council Highways Dept and the NWMBA for checking the book for errors and for pointing out how pending access changes may affect things in the future.

INTRODUCTION

Hi. Welcome to the North Wales Mountain Bike Guide.

The aim of this book is to lessen the impact of mountain biking in certain overused areas by showing that there are rides of equal quality away from those areas. Indeed some of the most enjoyable rides can be found in the outlying areas which are less used by walkers and cyclists alike.

North Wales is, as you are aware, a very popular recreational area, used by all sorts of people to satisfy their leisure needs; from climbers to canoeists to botanists to artists to paraponters to mountain bikers. This variety of use can cause conflicts and, as one of the latest groups to explore this area, we have come under criticism for causing damage and for reckless behaviour. This came to a head with the Snowdonia

National Park seeking an order permanently prohibiting cyclists from the bridleways of Yr Wyddfa (Snowdon) .

Snowdon Summertime Cycling Restrictions.
Following consultation with cycling organisations and the local NWMBA this has been modified into a voluntary restriction on riding all the Snowdon bridleways. This restriction covers all bridleways except the Maesgwm (Telegraph Valley) bridleway. The ban is in operation between the hours of 10 a.m. and 5 p.m. from the 1st of June to the 30th of September. The problems on Snowdon have been excessive speed on descending the mountain and trespass onto the Snowdon Railway which is not a right of way for cyclists (or walkers for that matter!). In order to address this problem it is important that cyclists are seen to show more mountain sense by restricting speed, following a sensible route and avoiding busy areas during the summer months. The mountains of North Wales are not a race track and should not be treated as such. It should be noted that restoration work on the Snowdon paths has been done to prevent erosion and **not** to make it easier for walkers and faster for mountain bikers.

CODES OF CONDUCT
The Mountain Bike Code
Only ride where you know you have legal right.

Always give way to horses and walkers.

Avoid animals and crops. In some circumstances this may not be possible, at which times contact should be kept to a minimum.

Take all litter with you.

Leave all gates as found.

Keep noise down.

Do not get annoyed with anyone; it never solves any problems.

Always try to be self-sufficient, for you and your bike.

Never create a fire hazard.

The Country Code
Enjoy the countryside and respect its life and work.

Guard against risk of fire.

Fasten all gates.

Keep your dogs under close control.

Keep to public paths across farmland.

Use gates and stiles to cross fences, hedges and walls.

Leave livestock, crops and machinery alone.

Take your litter home.

Help keep all water clean.

Protect wildlife, plants and trees.

Take special care on country roads.

Make no unnecessary noise.

Remember that the countryside is someone's workplace.

The Forest Code

Guard against all risks of fire, protect trees, plants and wildlife.

Leave things as you find them, take nothing away.

Keep dogs and animals under proper control.

Avoid damaging buildings, fences, hedges, walls and signs.

Leave no litter.

Respect the work of the forest.

Observe all signs, do not leave open or obstruct gates and for your own safety keep clear of forestry operations.

And finally, respect the peace and quiet of the forest and avoid disturbing others.

EQUIPMENT AND CLOTHING

The best way to carry everything that you feel is necessary is in a light rucksack or bum bag.

Maps:

The necessary 1:50 000 map is specified at the beginning of each route. The 1:25 000 scale large sheet maps are available for much of this area and should be used when possible.

Compass:

A good quality Silva compass and the ability to use it!

Whistle:

The international distress signal is six blasts in a minute followed by one minute's pause, then repeat.

Torch:
A headtorch is best to keep your hands free. The distress symbol is the same as for the whistle.

You may also feel it necessary to carry a survival blanket or bivvi bag.

Tool kit:
At the very least should contain the following;

Spare inner tube, valves, valve remover, puncture repair kit, pump, spare pump valve and tyre lever. Adjustable spanner. Allen keys to fit all parts of your bike. Crank remover. Chain splitter. Spoke key. Small screwdriver. Spare brake and gear cables.

This should cover emergency repairs but I often carry the following as well;

Swiss Army knife (for extracting scouts from horses hooves!)

8, 9 and 10 mm Y wrench (for pedals).

Spare ball bearings, various sizes.

Film case full of lithium grease.

Cone spanners.

Pliers.

Spare toe strap.

Some tape.

Small torch.

2 x jubilee clips.

Spare washer for flexstem.

Spare pair of brake blocks.

A high factor sunblock.

There is no better system than preventive maintenance. Get to know your bike, look after it, and it will look after you.

Bike:
The best you can afford!

Clothing:
I believe that a good mix of cycling clothes and climbing/walking clothes is the best way to keep safe and warm. A system of layers of thinner garments is best for regulating temperature. I used the following in various combinations during research for the guide and can thoroughly recommend them:

Lycra cycling shorts.

Been Bag cycling trousers. These are high cut at the back and keep the lower back and kidneys warm like no other outdoor trousers do - highly recommended.

Helly Hansen long-sleeved Lifa Thermal Vest.

Long and short-sleeved cycling tops.

Wrinkly Pinks Mountain Bike Jacket - warm and comfortable, recommended.

Light-weight walking boots such as Merrells or High Tec.

Thermal gloves and cycling gloves.

Fleece headband for keeping my ears warm under my cycling helmet. Colours are optional but I go for black and purple!

Helmet:

This item is the number one priority for mountain bikers. Get one as it will make you feel safer and this makes you more relaxed and that makes you ride better which then makes you less likely to fall off! Make sure it conforms to ANSI and/or SNELL safety standards.

Food:

I personally carry things like dried and fresh fruit (raisins, bananas, dates etc.), flapjack or muesli bars, Mars Bars or chocolate, and cheese and pickle sandwiches. Sometimes, if it is going to be a really long day, I might sneak in tins of beans and rice pudding! It is important to avoid just eating quick energy foods as your blood sugar level will peak and then drop quickly so some stodge is needed to keep you going in the long-term. The meal the night before is a good chance to stock up on carbohydrates like pasta, potatoes and bread to keep you ticking the next day.

Water:

Carry plenty, drink before you go and do not turn down a chance to refill your water bottle. I have found that cycling bottles tend to leak when in a rucksack and that a better choice is the Sig bottle (metal water bottle). The water is kept in my rucksack as I find that bottle cages get in the way when carrying.

SAFETY AND FIRST-AID

There are a few steps which you can take to make your trip safer;

1) Tell someone where you are going and when you should be back.

2) Go out in small groups rather than solo (5 or 6 maximum).
3) If you do go solo, take it easy.
4) Carry all necessary equipment including a first-aid kit.
5) Become more knowledgable about first-aid, bike mechanics and
   navigation.

First-aid, the best way to be of assistance to yourself and your friends in the event of an accident is to have completed one of the numerous St. John's first-aid certificates e.g. the Mountaineering First-aid Certificate.

The basic procedure with a conscious patient is to stop any bleeding by direct pressure and elevation. Then treat for shock i.e. make them comfortable, keep them warm and reassure them.

If they are unconscious make sure their airway is clear, that they are breathing and that they have a pulse. Then cover them and keep checking those three things. The best way to assist in this is by turning them to the recovery position. However, you should be very careful in doing this if there is the slightest risk of the patient having a spinal or neck injury. If you have to move an unconscious patient, get all the assistance you can and try not to bend or twist the back and neck.

If they have passed out from dehydration, exposure or any other non-impact related reason, they should be put in the recovery position and watched carefully.

Anyone who has passed out (however briefly) after an impact should be sent to hospital for 24 hours observation as concussion can become compression which may be fatal.

Only give liquid for dehydration and exposure. If you think that the injured party could be receiving treatment in 6 hours or less, do not give liquids. If you do you may delay a vital operation and in the case of head, chest and abdominal injuries you could be putting the patient at risk.

However, if the injuries are slight or it is likely to be many hours before help arrives, a warm drink will help with shock.

For broken bones the idea is to immobilise the joint above and below the site of the injury in order to assist in the patient's removal, to make them more comfortable and to prevent further injury. You will have to use what you have at hand, including the bike frame and pump!

If the injury is serious then send someone for help (two people would be best) with the following information:

1) How many people are injured.
2) What you think the injuries are.
3) What time the accident happened.
4) Where the injured party is - give a grid reference if possible.
5) Weather conditions/cloud base, as evacuation may be made by helicopter.
6) The names of the people in the party.

A very basic first-aid kit contains some sticky plasters, some bandages and a pair of scissors, as well as anything you can find in your rucksack.

If you think this is all complicated, then you are right. There is lots to learn so the best advice is to get yourself trained.

MAP WORK

This guide has been produced with the use of the Ordnance Survey Landranger 1:50 000 scale maps in mind. All the research was done using these maps and hopefully the route descriptions cover any inadequacies in this scale of map, the main one being that they do not show field boundaries.

It is worth noting that the larger scale 1:25 000 outdoor leisure sheets are available for much of this area. All grid references quoted will fit these maps which offer much more detail.

The first thing to say about Ordnance Survey (OS) maps is that the top of the map is always north. This is not so with the sketch maps in the guide itself due to the limited space on a page. The symbols used on OS maps are clearly described down the right side of each map though they do vary with the different series and scale of map - so if in doubt, check.

SCALE

The blue grid lines that run across the map's horizontal and vertical axes are 2 cm apart at this scale - 2 cm represents 1 km. So the distance either horizontally or vertically across a square is 1 km. If you cross diagonally the distance is closer to 1.5 km. The main use of grid lines and squares will be fully explained later.

With this scale in mind, a rider travelling at 10 km per hour will take 6 minutes to travel 1 km and cross one grid square - at 20 km per hour this will take 3 minutes. As the top and bottom speeds of a mountain biker are very far apart, probably between 5 kmph and 80 kmph, judging distance whilst on the move is very difficult. The best way to do this accurately is to invest in a cycle computer. This instrument is incredibly useful for navigating in remote areas.

Rights of Way

All rights of way are in red in this series of maps and cyclists generally have right of access to all but the red dotted lines of the footpath. This is based in law and the statutes are quite clear on this matter. Most people are aware of this and if you are seen riding on footpaths you will give us all a bad name and endanger future access to many areas. Rights of way do change and the only way of being 100% certain of a right of way's status is to consult the Definitive Maps which are held by the Local Highway Authority.

Contour lines

The contour lines in this series are at 10 m intervals and are a feature of maps which you will come to cherish. The closer together they are, the steeper the angle and the harder you must work to climb up the hillside.

However, it is not sufficient to leave it at that. There are two types of slope, namely concave and convex, and one is safer than the other when descending.

For descent, the concave slope is identifiable by contours which start close together and then spread out, offering a clear view of its slope and therefore any obstacles on it.

The convex slope is indicated by contours that start spread apart and then bunch together. This does not offer a view of its slopes and should be treated with caution as obstacles can appear with little or no warning.

Sometimes it is difficult to differentiate between ridge and valley, top and bottom. The solution is simple - find a river. I have yet to see one that runs along the brow of a ridge so water must be in the lower ground.

Map memory

One of the most useful skills to develop in relation to map work is a good map memory, i.e. the ability to store up a list of objects which you will pass and can tick off as you go. For example, cross the ford, climb the hill opposite, take second left, at the building bear right and turn left at the road etc.

This will save you reaching for the map or guide every time you reach a junction or feature. As you develop and learn to trust your map memory, you can add distances and more features.

However, if you are unsure or think that perhaps things have changed since the map was printed etc. then check before you go too far wrong.

The other feature of map reading is to learn to see the map in three dimensions and to imagine what it looks like for real. This may sound obvious but many people find this difficult. The amount of information on an OS map is fantastic and the better you learn to read and relate this information to the ground, the more chance you have of noticing when something is wrong.

Grid references

In order to use this guide correctly you will need to relate its information to the relevant OS map and this will often be done in the form of Grid References which will describe a road junction or the corner of a forest etc. This technique is not hard but can seem complicated to begin with, so prick up your ears and concentrate.

Pick up any map - there are blue grid lines that cross the map vertically and horizontally. The vertical lines are called eastings because they progress across the map from west to east and are numbered to represent this progression.

The horizontal lines are called northings because they progress across the map from south to north and are numbered to represent this progression. The lines are numbered along the edges of the map.

The first stage is to produce a four-figure grid reference or GR. The easiest way to do this is to pick any square on the map and mentally draw a capital L along its west and south borders. Now read off the numbers of these lines starting with the vertical easting, then the horizontal northing. In the example diagram this would give you the four figure GR of 27 34, i.e. the 1 km square with a telephone box and a church/chapel without spire or tower in it.

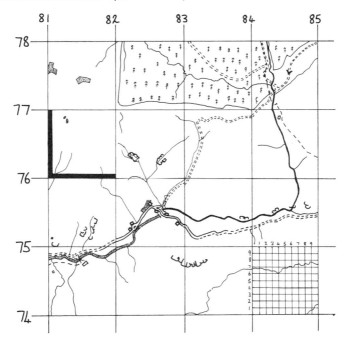

Unfortunately, this is rarely sufficient as 1 km square is a large area which may contain several similar features. It is therefore necessary to divide each of the axes into tenths which would give us 100 m squares. Then we need to describe which of the 100 m squares we are referring to e.g., 9 tenths across and three tenths up.

Locate the square GR 28 33 in the example diagram. Supposing we were to meet to swap tall mountain biking tales at one of the houses in this square. If I was to say we will meet at the house at GR 82 75 how would you know which one?

So, supposing I chose the house farthest north-east. In order to give you a six-figure GR for that house, I would have to estimate the tenths.

For the eastings it would be 28 and 7 tenths i.e. 287, and for the northings it would be 33 and 9 tenths i.e. 339. This would give us the six-figure GR 287 339. Still with me? Well done, I am glad someone is! So the description would be: Bodlas, the house overlooking the valley at GR 287 339.

One point which is important to remember is that the GR actually gives you the co-ordinates of the bottom left-hand corner of the square. From this you should mentally construct the rest of the square.

Try out this method a few times on the example below until you are happy with the system. There is a short description of how to construct GR's on the right-hand side of the OS maps.

COMPASS

The compass is an instrument which many people fear and which seems to have developed some sort of mystique. However once you get to grips with it you will see how simple it is to use and how useful it can be.

The most commonly used make of compass is the Silva compass. There are many types and they are not cheap. It is useful to buy one which has the added facilities of a magnifying glass and roamers for different scales of map.

The compass has two main functions: firstly to orientate the map and secondly to produce bearings for one purpose or another. It can also assist in the reading of the map and the production of accurate grid references or GR's.

The features of a compass are as follows;
1) Direction of travel arrow.
2) Magnifying glass.
3) Roamers.
4) Magnetic arrow.
5) Base plate arrow.
6) Scale in degrees on the compass housing.
7) Bearing reading point.

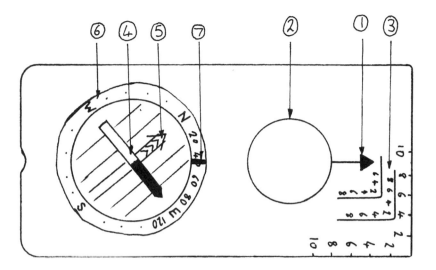

Diagram of compass with features numbered as on page 18.

Map orientation using the compass

This is a very simple operation that is immensely useful. Imagine that you know where you are but are having difficulty relating the map to the features on the ground. Or, that you have arrived at a multiple junction of tracks - you know on the map which one you want but in the heat of the moment you cannot remember which one you cycled down in real terms.

1) Hold out the map (folded to the area in which you are operating).
2) Place the compass on the map, not obscuring the relevant details, and aligned north.
3) Grip the map and compass together between the fore fingers and thumb of one hand.
4) Turn yourself round in a circle until the red end of the magnetic arrow points directly to the top (north) of the map.
5) The map is now orientated to the ground and all features can be related directly from their map position to their ground position.

19

Taking a bearing from the map

This is the main function of the compass and I will explain some of its many uses later - but first, how to do it!

1) Line up the direction of travel arrow with the intended route. It is best to use the edge of the compass rather than the actual direction of travel arrow as this tends to obscure the data on the map.

2) Holding the compass firmly in place, rotate the compass housing (which contains the scale in degrees) until you have the base plate arrow pointing to the north end of the map. The easiest way to do this is to line it up with the vertical grid lines on the map (eastings).

3) Lift the compass off the map and read the bearing where the direction of travel arrow crosses the compass housing, e.g. 076 degrees, then add five to it which makes 081 degrees. Do not just do it in your head - physically do it on the compass.

4) Holding the compass in your hand with the direction of travel arrow pointing away from you, turn round in a circle until the base plate arrow and the red end of the magnetic arrow are pointing in exactly the same direction.

5) Move off in the direction indicated by the direction of travel arrow, keeping the base plate arrow and magnetic arrow lined up at all times.

Five simple stages. Do not worry about the why of adding 5 degrees. This is to do with the difference between grid and magnetic north.

When you are following a bearing, the easiest way to move accurately is to spot a feature which lies along the line of the bearing, go to it and then repeat the process until you arrive in the vicinity of your target. Do not choose a sheep as your marker as they tend to move about!

The main reasons for following a bearing are because of poor visibility and to cross featureless ground. In this book there may be one or two occasions when the bridleway is so vague that you need to keep a check on the direction in which you are travelling in order to arrive at the next identifiable point. Also if you get caught out (Howzzat!) in poor light it is very easy to stray from the right track and therefore run the risk of getting lost.

Taking a bearing from the ground

There are often situations when you are able to see your target in the distance but know that either the cloud will soon obscure it or that darkness will do the same. In this situation it is useful to take a bearing to that object to ensure that you continue in the right direction.

1) Point the direction of travel arrow at the object as accurately as possible.

2) Rotate the compass housing until the base plate arrow is pointing in the same direction as the magnetic arrow.

3) Move off in the direction indicated by the direction of travel arrow, keeping the base plate arrow and the magnetic arrow lined up at all times.

There may be situations in which you wish to relate this information to the map, e.g., if you have made an error or are slightly lost, but think that you are on one of two bridleways and cannot decide which. Take a bearing down the line of the bridleway and then relate it to the map. Providing that the two routes are not parallel, this should help you to decide which one you are on.

To do this, follow the procedure for taking a bearing from the ground and then continue in the following manner;

4) Read off the bearing in degrees and then subtract five - again, physically remove five on the compass housing.

5) Place the compass on the map in the general area where you think you are and then rotate the compass until the base plate arrow is pointing to the north end of the map.

6) Line up the edge of the compass with the bridleways and hopefully one will lie roughly along the edge of the compass indicating that this is likely to be the one that you are on.

Note that this will only work if you **are** correct in the assumption of your general location.

Another use for the compass is for locating, for example, a junction in open country or on a ridge. If you are looking for the right place to start dropping off a ridge and you know from the map that there is an identifiable object somewhere, such as a house or an adjacent peak, then try this procedure.

1) Take a bearing on the map of that identifiable object visible from the point at which you need to drop off the ridge. Do not forget to add five degrees.
2) As you move along the ridge, line up the base plate arrow and the magnetic arrow and look to see if the direction of travel arrow is pointing at your chosen object.
3) When the direction of travel arrow does point at the object you then know that you are in the vicinity of the drop off point.

This method can help in the location of junctions etc. but beware - as with all things compass-wise, it is liable to pilot error and is only as accurate as you make it.

There are several good tips for helping with accurate compass work;
1) **Aiming off**: suppose you are cycling towards a forest that runs at right angles to your direction of travel in both directions. There is a gate into the forest which you want to find but it is very misty. If you were to take a bearing directly at the gate from a known position, the chances are that by the time you reached the forest you would be off to one side by a distance, and would not know which side. So if you build in an error by aiming off to the right by 200m when you reach the forest, you can turn left and follow the edge of the forest until you find the gate.
2) **Collecting features**: e.g. the join of two rivers. If you aim between the two then sooner or later you will reach the point where they meet and you will know where you are.
3) **Handrails**: e.g. the edge of a lake, or something which you know will lead to a certain point. Following one of these means that you can relax until you get there.
4) **Attack points**: often when trying to locate a specific feature it is best to use a collecting feature or handrail to get you close and then from this attack point try to find the feature. It is frequently better to go a little out of the way to make things easier, especially in poor visibility.

FOREST AREAS

Forest Enterprise (formerly the Forestry Commission) allows cycling on some of its land but is becoming worried because of the actions of a few mountain bikers who behave in a reckless manner;

a) Use of excessive speed in areas frequented by walkers and families. Please be aware of your speed and the fact that you can approach almost silently causing alarm to people who are out for a quiet walk etc. **You do not have right of way over walkers and horse-riders.**

b) Cyclists have been known to enter working areas of forest where there is a real danger of meeting heavy machinery or falling timber etc. If you see "Danger tree felling" signs then do not enter that area - it is in your best interest.

If accidents occur or complaints continue then Forestry Enterprise may take action to restrict mountain bike use within its forests in order to comply with Statutory Health and Safety Regulations.

There are four main forest areas in North Wales where mountain biking is encouraged and there are bike hire services available. These are:

Coed-y-Brenin Forest Park. Bikes and a map of routes are available from the visitor centre at Beics Coed Y Brenin GR 715 277 OS No 124 Dolgellau.

Beddgelert Forest. Bikes and a map are available from Beddgelert Bikes, Hafod Ruffydd Uchaf, at GR 569 495 OS No 115 Snowdon.

The forests around Betws-y-Coed. Bikes and a map are available from Beics Betws at the Visitor Centre at GR 795 564 OS No 115 Snowdon.

Clocaenog Forest near Rhuthin. There is no bike hire but this newly opened forest contains a long and difficult mountain bike route (not for beginners) well worthy of attention, as well as 400 km of forest road. Information from the visitor centre at GR 035 511 OS Landranger 116 Denbigh and Colwyn Bay area.

For further information you can phone Forest Enterprise on either (01341) 422 289 for Coed y Brenin area or (01492) 640 578 for the other areas.

If you decide to cycle in the forests of North Wales, it can be a good idea to talk to the bike hire people first as they are in touch with the authorities and should have up-to-date information about "no-go areas". You can also speak to Forestry Ventures direct on (01492) 640 578.

Forests are constantly changing as work within them progresses and they will have knowledge of these changes etc.

In addition, some areas of forest are closed for mountain bike and motorbike races as well as car rallies.

The forest routes in this guide are good examples of forest cycling and are all well worthwhile trips. However, they will also be subject to change and restrictions over the course of time so please check. You will be parking close to the hire centres so this does not require much effort and it could help avoid problems in the future.

One final note, I know that mountain bikers tend to go out in any weather but it may prove sensible (especially on the higher routes) to obtain a mountain weather forecast before setting out. This can be obtained either from the Warden Centre at Pen y Pass or by calling "Mountain Call" on (01891) 722 285.

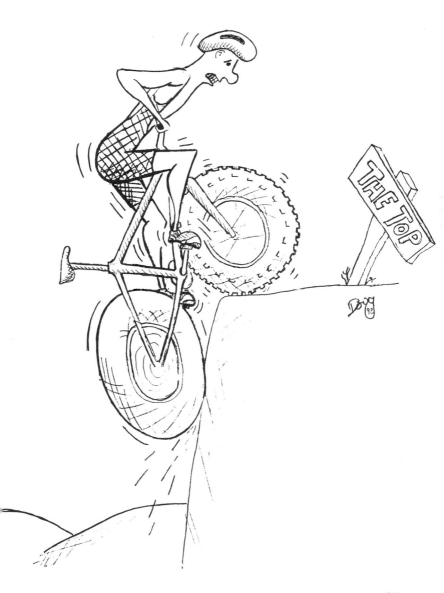

Route 1 - Llangollen

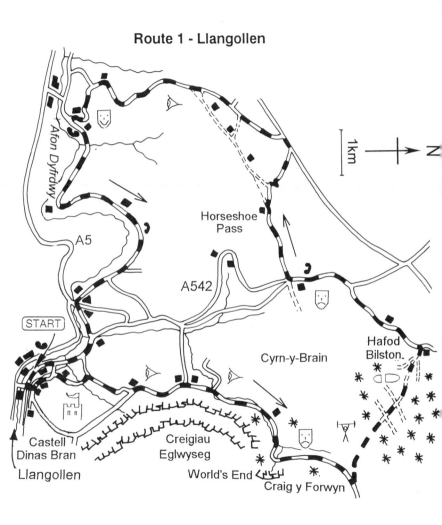

RUTHIN AREA

1. Llangollen

Llangollen, Eglwyseg valley, Craig y Forwyn, Hafod Bilston, Tan-y-foel, Craig-y-Rhos, Llangollen.

Map = OS nos. 116 Denbigh, 117 Chester and 125 Bala(!)
Best conditions = After hard frost
Length = 39km of which 8km are off road
Height Gain = 650m
Time = 3-5 hours
Stars = ⁴⁴

This good route starts from the main carpark in Llangollen at GR 214 420 (OS 117). It is mainly on minor roads (though many of these are very rough) with a short section of A-road. The views throughout are outstanding with forests, cliffs, mountains and moorland. The climbs are not tough (except for one!) and towards the end there is an excellent descent on winding minor roads. Generally traffic-free and a worthwhile trip despite being on the border of three maps!

From the carpark in the centre of Llangollen at GR 214 420 turn right towards the main street and then left along it and over the bridge over the Afon Dyfrdwy (River Dee). At the T-junction at the end of the bridge turn right and then immediately left, to the right of the Bridge End Hotel (the house with the turrets).

Climb over the canal and fork left in front of the school (views of town falls which is a favourite place for canoeists to swim!) before heading out into the hills. Climb two short hills along narrow lanes with views of Castell Dinas Bran. At 2.14km and GR 213 435, turn right towards Minerva and World's End.

This road leads you through the beautiful Eglwyseg valley with French style limestone cliffs on the right. At 3.4km you bear left with the road and shortly afterwards drop down into the valley bottom. Bear right over a bridge just beyond a farmyard at 5.03km and wind along the valley floor. At GR 229 479 (7.93km) you pass an old Elizabethan-style house and farm on a short new section of road.

From here there is a great view up the valley to Craig Y Forwyn (Crag of the Maiden) which you soon climb to. The road swings sharply left and heads due north. Cross the ford and then tackle the only steep hill of the day which brings you out of the forest and onto the moors. Follow the road up to the brow of the hill (with wide views to the rear or should that be views of the wide rear!). Just as you get views to the north you reach a wooden signpost on the left of the road at GR 236 495 and 10.34km.

Turn left onto the bridleway and ride into the moors. You will find that the first section of moorland is very muddy and you should carry over the worst sections to avoid further damage and to keep your drive system in working order! However, if you do this ride after several days of hard frost you may well have no such problem. You will reach the forest at 11.75km at a double gate and stile. Go straight into the forest along a narrow, recently cleared track passing over forest roads at 11.96km and 12.36km.

The following section is also the line of Offa's Dyke LDP, so look out for walkers and give way to them.

The bridleway status is in the process of being diverted along forest tracks in order to separate walkers from horses and bikes. If you see new bridleway signs indicating the new route then you must follow them as the original route will by then have been downgraded to footpath. At the time of writing this has not happened, but it is expected in the near future.

The third section of track has some interesting pallet steps which you can clear if you try, and then you drop to a narrow bridge (beware) at 13.11km.

Turn left along the dike edge for 30m before dropping to the right down a narrow path with some extremely technical bits. These will only be cleared by those with a good eye and a technical bent. This soon eases and you cross a third forest road at 13.57km and drop to two gates. Take the left-hand gate continuing down a narrow path until you pass through the corner of a garden at Hafod Bilston and out of their gate to reach the road. Do not worry - it is a right of way!

Turn left climbing past a gallery/studio and along a rough minor road. At GR 194 496 you reach the A542 Horseshoe Pass road and turn left up it. Climb to 17.85km and GR 192 482 where you turn right onto a minor road just before a sign to the Ponderosa Café. Drop through some quarry workings to reach a house at the back of a ravine/gully. Continue round the valley side keeping to the minor road and following it down to the A5104. Turn left along this road for 350m then turn left again up the first minor road.

Climb the hill keeping to the surfaced road (good views) and over the top before dropping down the far side in some style with good views back to Castell Dinas Bran. Please do not take any short-cuts across the mountainside as there is conservation work being done in the area. After a short climb there is a section down to a fork in the road just beyond a cattle grid at 26.4km (GR 147 438 on OS 125). Take the left-hand road and make a short climb before dropping along the narrow road round the back of Craig-y-Rhos through a farm (beware there may be a closed gate here!). Continue down through some corners until you arrive at a T-junction by a phone box at 30.07km

Turn left and drop some more before undulating along the valley bottom, passing the aptly named "Conquering Hero" pub at 33.1km and reaching a T-junction at 36.4km and GR 190 444. Turn right and follow this road into Llangollen then turn right over the bridge at 38.6km to reach the carpark at 39km.

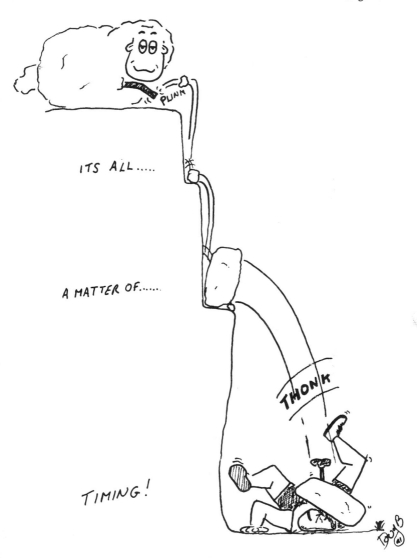

Looking towards Craig y Forwyn.

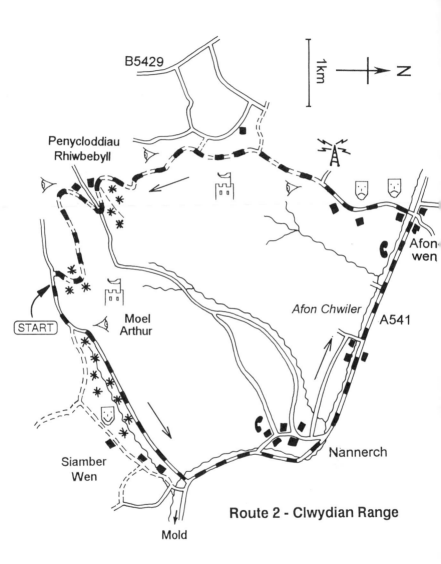

B5429

1km

N

Penycloddiau
Rhiwbebyll

Moel
Arthur

START

Siamber
Wen

Afon
wen

Afon Chwiler

A541

Nannerch

Mold

Route 2 - Clwydian Range

2. Clwydian Range

Moel Arthur, Afon Wen, Nant Coed-y-mynydd, Rhiwbebyll, Moel Arthur.

Map = OS no. 116 Denbigh
Best conditions = During dry period
Length = 21.5km of which 9km are off road
Height gain = 400m
Time = 1.5 - 3 hours
Stars = **

This route starts from the small carpark below Moel Arthur at GR 146 657. The off-road riding is mostly on grassy tracks which does make the going quite hard in places though it is never extreme. There is one killer hill to take on and a middle ring ascent of this would be impressive. Good views throughout.

From the carpark at Moel Arthur at GR 146 657, turn left and cycle north-east through the col with some wide views. You will soon be enjoying a long, steep and narrow downhill section which leads to the A541 at 4.04km. Here you turn left. The A541 drops gently most of the way to Afon Wen and you may have that uncomfortable feellng that so far it has all been too easy!

At 10.73km turn left in Afon Wen heading towards the Craft and Antiques Centre but keep to the road and begin to climb the horrendously gnarly hill ahead. Get into the lowest of the low gears and try to think of something distracting as you grind up finally to reach a right-angled bend at 12.40km. As I said, a middle chainring ascent of this hill would be something to write home about!

From the right-angled bend where the road turns towards the TV mast at GR 126 700, go straight on along the rough track which heads generally south. At 13.63km you reach a staggered + junction above Nant Coed-y-mynydd where you go straight on through a gate following the bridleway sign. On a note of caution - these tracks are in fact byways so you may encounter vehicles.

Ignore a right turn at 14.76km continuing along the good track which starts to descend. Just beyond some gates you reach a fork at the edge of a forest at 17.1km. The left option is also a bridleway but our route takes you through a gate on the main track and down to a road at 17.61km.

Turn left round the valley above Rhiwbebyll for 70m before taking the first right turn along a track which leads you through a gate and behind some ruined buildings. The track gets steadily muddier and there is some climbing to a gate at 18.15km. Beyond this you continue to climb (which can be hard work due to the mud) until you cycle round the back of Glyn Arthur valley at 19.89km and reach a minor road at 20.57km and GR 141 656.

Turn left and float up the smooth tarmac which feels wonderful after the clingy mud of the last few kilometres. At 21.25km go over a cattle grid at the col between Moel Arthur and Moel Llys-y-coed. Turn left into the carpark and that's it! You may wish to take a walk up Moel Arthur for the wide view from its summit and to unwind those tired legs. Now it is time to toss a coin to see who is unlucky enough to have to drive back down the hill and who gets to ride!

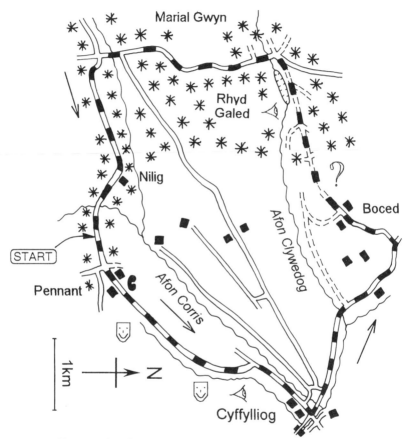

Route 3 - Clocaenog Forest

3. Clocaenog Forest

Nilig, Cyffylliog, Tai-isaf, Boced, Llyn Clywedog, Nilig.

Map = OS no. 116 Denbigh and Colwyn Bay
Best conditions = Any, but particularly good in the snow
Length = 17km of which 14km are on very minor roads
Height gain = 350m.
Time = 1.5 - 2.5 hours
Stars = **

This fairly gentle route starts from the grassy lay-by near the bridge inside the forest at GR 026 546. It passes through some wild scenery and pleasant forest. The views are generally good over the Clwydian Range on one side and into Snowdonia on the other. If the weather is bad in Snowdonia it is often worthwhile breaking away from the mountains and their grip on the clouds to visit this area. The forest is host to a number of motorbike events and major car rallies including the RAC Rally, so roads may be closed at times for public safety.

From the grassy lay-by inside the forest to the east of Nilig at GR 026 546 head east over the bridge climbing gently to a crossroads (phone). Go straight over the junction and continue, heading north-east now, past Pennant. Follow this minor road as it drops to a T-junction. Turn right and cycle into the village of Cyffylliog - beware blind bends, Landrovers and Ivor Williams trailers (you won't dent these!). In Cyffylliog, take the second left just before the river at 5.4km towards Nantglyn. Follow the river until the road bears right up a short hill before heading pleasantly along the side of the valley.

Pass a dead-end road on the left at 7.6km (do not try to take the obvious short-cut bridleway up to the left as it becomes a jungle before too long). Drop a short way before climbing steeply to Tai-isaf farm. Beyond this large farm the road levels and you take the next dead-end road on the left at 8.48km and GR 038 592.

Climb steeply past two farms on an easy road until it becomes a track and you reach a fork at 9.83km. Take the right fork which leads you behind some cattle sheds, through a gate and up to the end of the track at a line of trees at 10km and GR 028 581. At this point you have an excellent view of the Clwydian Range to the east.

Note: please take care whilst cycling through this next section as this field may be used during lambing for pregnant ewes. Keep your speed down!

From the end of the track in the field continue in your present direction diagonally across the field (which actually is a byway) until you reach a gate at 10.36km some 50m down from the top corner of the field. Go through the gate and along the narrow path beside the forest beyond until you reach a gate into the forest at 10.8km.

Go straight into the forest ignoring turnings to either side until you reach and cross a forest road at 11.36km. Follow the rutted wet track on the opposite side of the road up and then trickily down to emerge at Llyn Clywedog at 12.05km. You may wish to divert to the water's edge as this is an excellent food stop and viewpoint. Sooner or later follow the main track to the right along the lakeside until you reach a metalled road at 12.56km and GR 006 574.

Turn left when you meet this road following it up a steep hill and out of the forest. You will continue along the edge of some moorland before dropping into the forest again beside a cleared area. There are some good views of the Clwydian range from here. Keep going to an obvious crossroads where the road on which you are travelling has priority at 14.43km. Turn left pausing only to look back into North Wales before climbing a short hill which leads to a long, gentle descent all the way back to your car at 16.63km.

If you wish to do a much harder route there is a long ride set by Forestry Ventures - details from the Visitor Centre in the forest (GR 035 512). It is a difficult route and you are guaranteed to get wet and muddy so you must be properly equipped.

Looking along Llyn Clywedog

Route 4 - Mynydd Mynyllod

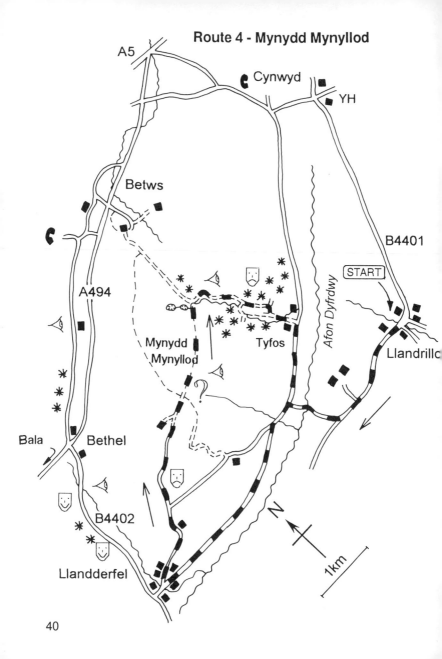

BALA AREA

4. Mynydd Mynyllod

Tyfos, Llandderfel, Cistfaen, Mynydd Mynyllod, Tyfos, Llandrillo.

Map = OS no. 125 Bala and Lake Vyrnwy
Best conditions = Cool summer evenings
Length = 17km of which 12km are on minor roads
Height gain = 300m
Time = 1-2 hours
Stars = *

This short route starts from the carpark next to the playground in Llandrillo at GR 035 371. It uses some rough and grassy tracks as well as quiet country lanes to give a fine ride in a picturesque area. There is one steep hill and the nature of the tracks makes this a slightly harder route than its length would suggest. The views are wide and uninterrupted for much of the route and the area is very quiet.

From the carpark next to the playground in Llandrillo at GR 035 371 head onto the main road and turn right over the bridge. Follow this road for 1.35km where you take the second right (not the one that leads to the sawmill). This road leads you over the river and through the old railway to a T-junction at 2.21km. Here you should turn left following the undulating road until you reach the village of Llandderfel. Here you take the first right at 6.05km (house with blue fence) and begin to climb to the north-east. Take the first left at 6.23km and continue the long climb above the River Dee with some good views.

After a long climb you will reach the end of the road at a gate at GR 998 386 and 8.87km. Follow the track beyond the gate ignoring a turning to Cistfaen cottage at 8.99km. Climb to a fork at 9.05km where you bear right along the remains of a wall. This track will soon get vague but do not panic - simply follow the line you are on to reach a gate in front of a small hill at 9.55km. Go through the gate bearing left round the hill and then back right after 50m. Climb the grassy track until you reach a gate onto the moors.

Go through the gate heading along the better track to reach another gate with an excellent panoramic view at 9.87km. Go through this gate following a Landrover track through the heather until it forks (not marked on OS) at 9.98km. Take the right fork which is easily missed.

Note: if you reach a 90 degree left bend then you know that you have missed the fork. Go back and try again!

Go through this gate heading along the edge of a field overlooking Llyn Mynyllod until you rejoin a track and are able to turn right through a gate just before a ford at 11.54km.

Cycle through the ford, through a gate and above a clearing to reach a gate into the forest at 12.6km. Go into the forest dropping to a sharp right-hand bend at 12.81km. Turn left here down a rough track instead of going round the bend (in one sense or other!). Judder down to a gate above a clearing at 12.99km and then continue the process until you reach a T-junction above a farm at 13.32km. Turn left through the farm then at the road turn right to Tyfos.

Follow the road along the valley side to 15.06km where you turn first left retracing your steps to the main road at 15.9km. Turn left heading back to Llandrillo which you soon reach to regain the carpark at 17.21km.

Dropping towards Tyfos Farm

Route 5 - Bwlch Maen Gwynedd

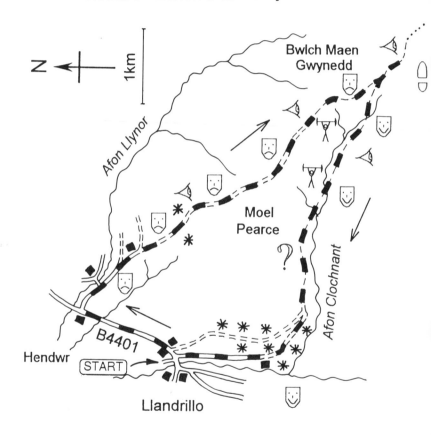

5. Bwlch Maen Gwynedd

Llandrillo, Moel Pearce, Bwlch Maen Gwynedd, Blaen-y-dre, Llandrillo.

Map = OS no. 125 Bala
Best conditions = After dry period
Length = 16km of which 3km are on roads
Height gain = 600m
Time = 2-4 hours
Stars = **

This quiet little route starts from the carpark in Llandrillo at GR 035 371. The entire ride is on grassy tracks which makes the going harder. The situation is remote and the views are wild - a very worthwhile afternoon's work.

Please be aware that there are a number of wet sections which you must carry over to avoid damage. This ride passes through areas which are Sites of Special Scientific Interest/National Nature Reserve (SSSI/NNR) status and should only be ridden by those sympathetic to the work of these foundations.

From the carpark at the riverside in Llandrillo at GR 035 371, turn left towards Cynwyd and Corwen. Cycle pleasantly along the B4401 for 1.68km until it is possible to turn right opposite Hendwr campsite up a dead-end road past a telephone. Climb gently to a wide fork at 2.17km where you bear right. Climb more steeply now, past a farm on the left at 2.34km, getting into bottom gear and grinding upwards.

After a difficult fight you reach a gate at 3.06km. Take a quick breather then carry straight on heeding the "Please keep on the road sign" up a rough track to the left of a wall. This has its very steep moments but is rideable all the way as you pass next to a small

45

forest at 4km. From the top of the trees continue up the now grassy track towards Moel Pearce. There is a short, easy-angled section leading to a gate at 4.76km and beyond this is a short, wet section where you must carry to prevent further erosion. Climb steeply up the flanks of Moel Pearce with good, wide views to a level section at a gate at 5.58km. Make the most of the short respite since there is one more steep section to come as you fight up towards the cairn on Bwrdd Arthur. You thankfully top out a little lower at 6.6km to be rewarded with a fine view of the Berwyns and, dare I say it, a short descent!

Drop the single track and undulate along some fun ruts and bumps for 1km until the final hill calls. Carry up the steep last section of this so as to avoid damaging the track, to reach the gate at Bwlch Maen Gwynedd at 7.94km. The bridleway continues over the col then to the right and up to the next col at 8.61km. However, if you wish to visit it and enjoy its view across Craig Berwyn, you must **walk** there and back as this is a Site of Special Scientific Interest/National Nature Reserve. If you do go, you will return to your bikes at 9.34km. Now for the restful return leg.

Drop back down the slope - instead of bearing right back the way you came, continue straight down to the right of the stream at 9.5km. Cross a small stream at 9.92km after 100m of carrying over a small wet patch, then repeat the process at 10.63km. Climb a narrow path to join a wider track which comes down to meet you and bear left along it at 10.8km. Roll easily down to reach a wood at 11.46km and GR 058 349 above the Clochnant river.

Take care to pass under the eaves of the trees and not to drop down to the stream and you will safely reach a stile/gate at 11.7km. Cross the stile following the path down for a short way then back up until you are level with the stile again at 11.89km. From here bear left along a vague path which leads directly from the stile. Follow this vaguely and not so vaguely through the heather. At 12.15km you reach a large bog just after a large, flat boulder on the right of the path. Carry over the bog then continue along the path as it drops towards a stile on the opposite side of the valley. Soon, however, the path bears right to reach the head of a rough track at 12.88km. You follow this to the right and a gate and bridleway sign at 13.32km.

Go through the gate before dropping down the track for 20m. Turn right through a gate and follow an old track through a field with low broken walls on either side. Follow this to a gate just above a forest at GR 038 356. Go through the gate and continue down into the forest ignoring a right turn along the forest edge. Drop roughly through the trees to a + junction at 14.3km where you go straight over and out of the forest to follow its lower edge. The views now open out towards your destination at Llandrillo.

Keep to the edge of the trees as you drop, bearing right at a fork near a large sycamore. Climb gently for a few metres then continue down, leaving the edge of the trees at the second gate. Pass a farmhouse on the left before joining the metalled road at a gate just beyond at 15.5km. Breeze along the road turning left then left again onto the B4401. 50m down the road turn right just before the bridge into the carpark at GR 035 371 and 16.2km.

Route 6 - Lake Vyrnwy Circuit

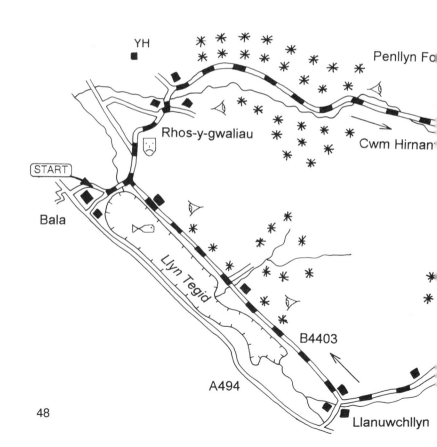

N ← | 1km

YH

Penllyn Fo

Rhos-y-gwaliau

Cwm Hirnan

START

Bala

Llyn Tegid

B4403

A494

Llanuwchllyn

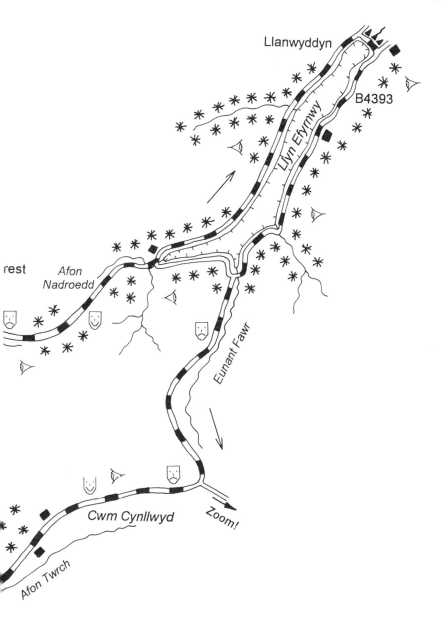

Llanwyddyn

B4393

Llyn Efyrnwy

rest

Afon
Nadroedd

Eunant Fawr

Cwm Cynllwyd

Zoom!

Afon Twrch

49

6. Lake Vyrnwy Circuit

Bala, Rhos-y-Gwaliau, Cwm Hirnant, Pen Bryn-y-fawnog, Ffridd Wydd-afon, Llyn Efyrnwy, Pont Eunant, Bwlch y Groes, Cwm Cynllwyd, Llanuwchllyn, Llangower, Bala.

Map = OS no. 125 Bala and Lake Vyrnwy
Best conditions = Any
Length = 58km, entirely on roads
Height gain/loss = 340m
Time = 2.5 - 4 hours
Stars = **

This route starts from the town of Bala at GR 925 360 on the A494. It is entirely on roads, the vast majority of which are narrow mountain and country lanes. It goes through an area which has no other rights of way for the cyclist and is extremely restricted for the walker. The area is varied, beautiful and generally very quiet: a very enjoyable route for mountain bikers and tourers alike.

From any of the carparks in Bala (GR 925 360), follow the B4391 south towards Llandrillo. Having crossed the bridge at the foot of the lake, climb a short way up a steepening hill and take the first right turn towards the village of Rhos-y-gwaliau.

Soon you will drop down a short, steep hill before gliding through the village to bear sharp left over a bridge in the valley bottom. (Rhos-y-gwaliau YHA first left once over the bridge). From here follow this road south-east along the riverside through the charming Cwm Hirnant (valley of the long stream). Soon you leave (leaf?) the trees and begin to climb across the open hillside. The hillside here is good for bilberries and, in the winter, for poly-bagging!

The hill is easier than it looks, except for the last 100m. Once over the top the descent is wonderfully flowing and steep. However, if you are with a young family then it would be sensible to keep close control over the youngsters, as the road is narrow and there is little room to avoid oncoming vehicles. Having left the village some 13.86km behind you will reach a T-junction at GR 964 242. Turn to the left pleasantly following the edge of Llyn Efyrnwy or Lake Vyrnwy. There are numerous picnic spots by the water's edge amongst some of the largest and oldest fir trees that I have ever seen.

Having cycled 8.7km with virtually no effort at all you will reach the dam wall at GR 019 193. Turn right over it, no doubt pausing to look over both sides at the contrasting views. At the opposite side of the dam you should turn right - but as there are some Tea Rooms on the left, a short diversion may be necessary! Follow the lakeside back up the valley for 7.4km to a junction at GR 962 224. Turn left towards Dinas Mawddwy and follow the road through high moorland for 6km until you reach a lonely junction and a wooden cross at GR 914 228.

To the left is the road to Dinas Mawddwy and one of the most obscene descents in the UK with an average angle of 5:1 and 10 chevrons in just 2km! Only speed freaks and the terminally brain dead need apply!

Our route is to the right and only one chevron to the top. The view, from both the junction and the top, is impressive as is the descent towards Llanuwchllyn. Though fast, this is a little safer than the previous descent as you can see further and there is room to pass oncoming vehicles. (G = 9.81m per square second and don't you just love it when it is on your side!)

Follow this road down to a T-junction at GR 881 298 just outside Llanuwchllyn, some 9km from the last one. Turn right onto the B4403, cruising gently along the side of Llyn Tegid, passing several more picnic spots and viewpoints. Finally you will reach a junction with the B4391 at GR 930 350 where you turn left and return to Bala.

Lake Vyrnwy

Route 7 - Coed Gordderw

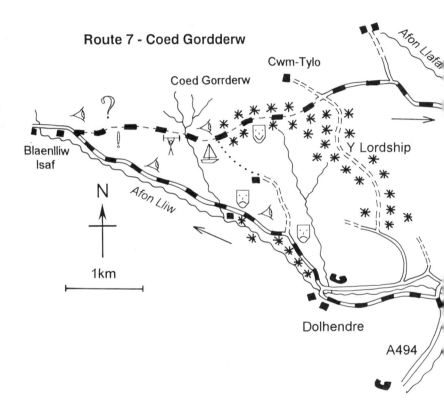

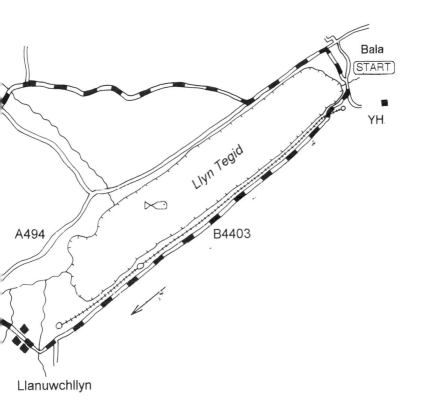

Bala

START

YH

Llyn Tegid

A494

B4403

Llanuwchllyn

55

7. Coed Gordderw

Bala, Llanuwchllyn, Dolhendre, Blaenlliw Isaf, Ffridd Trawsgoed, Coed Gordderw, Parc, Llanycil, Bala.

Map = OS no. 125 Bala and Lake Vyrnwy
Best conditions = After several hard frosts
Length = 33km of which 6km are off road.
Height gain = 350m
Time = 2.5 - 5 hours
Stars = **

This interesting and varied route starts from one of the many carparks in the town of Bala, GR 925 360 and is a great mix of picturesque lakeside meanderings and remote, wild moorland. It has a feeling of remoteness about it as it passes over the moors which is in stark contrast to the holiday feeling given by the lake road.

From any of the carparks in Bala at GR 925 360, head towards the north-eastern corner of the lake. Bear right along the lakeside once over the bridge, on the B4403. Pass the yacht club and ramble easily along the quiet road for 8km until you leave the lake and reach Llanuwchllyn. Keep on the B4403 as it turns sharp right until you reach the A494. Turn right along this then first left after 250m before a bridge on a bend. Follow this road for a further 2km or so until you bear right in the tiny village of Dolhendre and drop to a telephone box at a T-junction at GR 853 308. You have now come about 12km into the route but as this depends on which carpark you managed to park in, I will start the detailed description from the telephone box.

From the telephone box in Dolhendre at GR 853 308, turn left up the valley along the road heading north-west below the impressive Castell Carndochan cliffs. Climb the steep hill beside the forest (this should get you warmed up nicely!).

Continue pleasantly beyond the hill with some good views over to the Arans then drop to a gate at a farm called Buarthmeini (nice waterfalls to the left). Beyond the farm is a second steep hill to climb and then the road continues gently up above the Afon Lliw until you reach a third gate overlooking Blaenlliw Isaf farm at 5.75km. This distance is from the Dolhendre telephone box.

20m before the gate a line of rushes climbs the mountainside to the right. This is the beginning and vaguest part of the bridleway. Head up to the right of the rushes and probably surprise yourself by riding almost all the way to the small col above. Once over the col, bear left round the back of the marshy area and follow the improving track up through a cutting at 6.25km and another some 200m beyond.

Just beyond the second cutting you reach the brow of the hill (Bryn Cau) with some great views. From here you cycle down the grassy track heading for the track which climbs obviously up the opposite hillside beyond the Afon Erwent. At 7.15km you reach an old wooden gate close to the river. Cross to this and then head rightwards along the bank until you find a suitable crossing place at approximately 7.35km (preferably to the right of a small stream which joins the main river).

Climb the hillside beyond along a narrow path until you reach the top at 7.7km. Here the track improves vastly and the panorama is superb. Drop down the hillside beyond until the track forks at 8.2km some 400m from the forest. Take the left fork and follow this to a gate into the forest at 8.65km.

Go into the open forest. Follow the track along the left edge of the clearing past some pools and then along the right-hand side of a dry-stone wall. The wall leads you down through some heather until at 9.7km the track bears left through a hole in the wall (remains of old gate) overlooking the lower part of the forest (Coed Gordderw) and Cwm-Tylo farm.

Go through the hole in the wall then bear immediately right and head down the fire-break, ignoring the obvious track leading straight on. Watch out for a couple of deep ditches which cross the fire-break and reach the corner of the forest at a gate and stile at 10.25km. Go over the stile and continue along the edge of the forest until you reach a road at 10.65km. From here you have a number of choices of how to return to Bala. The most logical route is to follow the road east, bearing left into and through Parc after 3km. Follow this road (ignoring a left turn just outside the village) to Llanycil and the A494(T). Here you turn left towards Bala which you reach after a 1km. Now all you have to do is find the right car in the right carpark!

'GIAT NO CLINCIOLO'

Route 8 - Mawddach Estuary

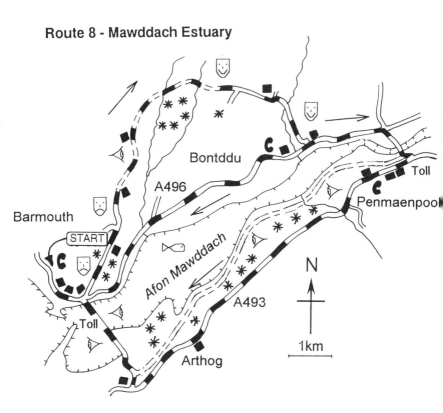

BARMOUTH AREA

8. Mawddach Estuary

Barmouth, Llwyn Onn, Sylfaen, Uwch-mynydd, Bontddu, Barmouth.

Map = OS no. 124 Dolgellau
Length = 20km, 3-4km off road
Height gain/loss = 300m
Time = 1.5 - 3 hours
Stars = **

Who planned upon this mountain's rock to build
High over the shifting sands of Mawddach´s flood.
They knew the soul of man had need of food
From heaven and that the world's creator willed.
That from hidden depths should hearts be thrilled
With touch of oceans wild infinitude.
They drank the dews of morning as they stood
And with the sunsets latest awe were thrilled.
H.D.R. 30/10/1891

**This route wanders around the beautiful Mawddach estuary
starting and ending in Abermaw or Barmouth as it is commonly
known. Barmouth is the home of the Three Peaks Yacht Race
and of the late famed adventurer H. W. Tilman. The riding is
mostly on roads and tracks though there are some rough, wet
bits. There are several ways back depending on time and fatigue.
The views are wide and excellent with mountains, forests and
the ever-present estuary.**

The front of Barmouth is one long line of carparks and any one will do as a start point. I will begin from the Sports Centre at GR 612 157. From here, head southwards towards the harbour, passing through this then reaching a T-junction after 580m. Turn right before climbing a short hill past Free Wales Rock. On your left will now be a long terrace. At the end of the terrace turn left at 1.03km and climb steeply, passing in front of the Panorama Hotel. Follow the road up through trees and then along the left side of a small valley to a junction and carpark at 2.4km and GR 624 166. Steeply up to the left after 1km is Barmouth Slabs, which is an excellent rock-climbing area for beginners. Our route lies straight on up the valley, which is called Llwyn Onn.

Climb a short, steep section and pass by a small farm on the right. At 3.4km the view opens up over the estuary and Dyffwys. Continue along a flat section passing by a second farm before climbing steeply again towards a farm called Sylfaen. Just beyond a gate the road drops gently to the farm. At this point - 4.63km and GR 630 184 - you must bear left off the road and onto a track which passes along the edge of an enclosure usually full of silage bales (big black bin bags!). Climb the track to reach a gate through a large stone wall at 4.82km. Follow the track beyond across the hillside passing through a number of gates to a fork in the track at 6.04km. Take the left-hand (upper) fork which leads through more gates. At 6.48km you leave the main track, dropping to the right to a gate at 6.5km. Go through the gate before heading over to the corner of a forest. Cross a couple of streams to reach the forest (Cerrig y Cledd) at a gate at 6.71km and GR 639 202.

Splash and gulp your way along the wet, muddy track which follows the edge of the trees for 300m. Continue down the track to a stream (Afon Dwynant) at 7.53km. Climb the grassy track beyond to reach the top of the hill at a gate and stile at 8.45km. Beyond this the track winds tightly down to the top of a road at 8.8km. Bear left which leads you quickly downhill, but beware of cars and two cattle grids on the narrow road. At 11.33km you will reach the A496 at Bontddu Hall (GR 673 189).

From here you have two options: either turn right along the road which leads easily back to Barmouth at 20km, or turn left following

The first descent of the route

the road until you can turn right to cross the Penmaenpool toll bridge. The George III on your right is very hospitable with good food and beer. From here, make your way along the estuary road until it is possible to turn right towards Morfa Mawddach Station (British Rail sign at the junction). At the station, follow the sandy track towards Barmouth Bridge (toll) and from the far end of this, turn left back into Barmouth at 26km.

Route 9 - Circuit of Cadair Idris

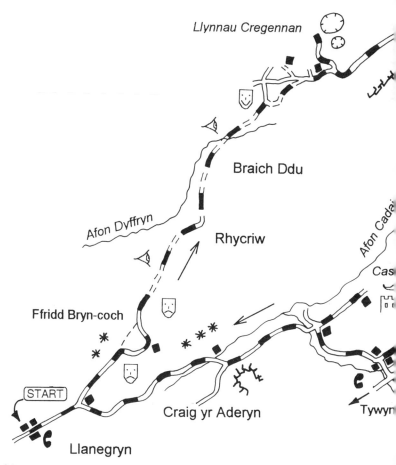

Llynnau Cregennan

Braich Ddu

Afon Dyffryn

Rhycriw

Afon Cada

Cas

Ffridd Bryn-coch

START

Craig yr Aderyn

Tywyn

Llanegryn

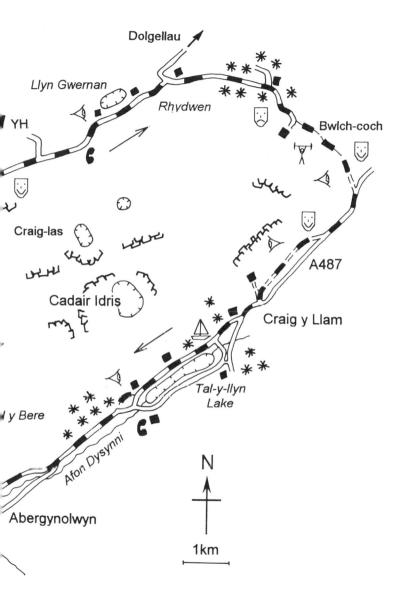

Dolgellau

Llyn Gwernan

YH

Rhydwen

Bwlch-coch

Craig-las

A487

Cadair Idris

Craig y Llam

Tal-y-llyn Lake

y Bere

Afon Dysynni

Abergynolwyn

N

1km

65

9. Circuit of Cadair Idris

Llanegryn, Ffridd Bryn-coch, Cwm-llwyd, Ffordd Ddu, Llynnau Cregennen, Llyn Gwernan, Rhydwen, Bwlch-côch, Mynydd Gwerngraig, Bwlch Llyn Bach, Tal-y-llyn Lake, Abergynolwyn, Pont Ystumanner, Pont y Garth, Llanegryn.

Map = OS no. 124 Dolgellau
Best conditions = Fine days to enjoy the views
Length = 53.5km of which 35km are on narrow lanes
Height gain/loss = 900m
Time = 5-8 hours
Stars = **

This route starts from the village of Llanegryn a few kilometres north of Tywyn on the A493 at GR 601 054. Cadair Idris (the chair of Idris) is one of the highest Welsh mountains and commands a spectacular position high above the beautiful Mawddach estuary. This route circumnavigates the mountain on roads and tracks giving stunning views of the mountains, valleys and estuaries that surround it. There is a large amount of climbing to be done but the situation and character of the route make that more than worthwhile. An excellent base for this and other routes in the area is Robin and Rosie's camping barn, Glanmorfa Bach, Llanegryn, (01654) 710 959.

Start from the carpark next to the bridge at the bottom of the village at GR 601 054. Though you could start from any point on the route, it is preferable to cycle clockwise around the mountain as this gives the best cycling. Turn right out of the carpark heading north-east away from the village on a straight, level road for 1.2km. At Bryn-gwyn the road bends right and a single-track road heads off leftwards up the hillside behind the house. Take the left-hand route.

The hill is called Ffridd Bryn-coch and it climbs non-stop for a cruel 4km! Struggle up this to a gate at the end of the road. Take a rest here before crossing the watershed and entering the hidden valley beyond. You are now on the old Monk's road, Ffordd Ddu (The Black Road). Follow it through the valley for 3km until you climb gently out at its far end to be greeted by a sudden wide view over the Mawddach estuary towards Barmouth. Keep to the track and roll downhill for 3km with a few gates (one hidden just round a bend) until you join a tarred minor road at GR 656 133.

Turn right onto the road and immediately go through a gate. Continue on for 500m to a junction. Here the route goes straight on but it is well worthwhile turning right and diverting to the Cregennen lakes 1km away. Having idled away some time at this peaceful spot return to the junction and continue north-east along the minor road as it drops into the valley beyond. Glide (mostly) for 7km. 1km after passing the Gwernan Lake Hotel, you turn right at Rhydwen, GR 714 167 (on the outside of a bend next to a house). Follow this single-track road pleasantly through woods and fields for 3km to a T-junction. Turn right here and fight your way up a number of short but very steep hills. After 1km of this the road drops for a few metres before turning sharp right to Maes Coch farm GR 743 158.

The next section will require some concentration to navigate correctly. From the outside of the sharp right bend, continue straight on through a gate. 20m beyond this go over a stile. Take the narrow track beyond as it passes between two stone walls and then follow the right-hand wall to a gate. 50m beyond the gate is a footpath sign nailed to a tree (rough justice in these parts!). Turn left and follow the small stream uphill for 150m to a vague junction. At the junction turn right fording the stream to reach a gate on the opposite bank. Pass through the gate then cross the field heading slightly upwards to reach a gate and stile. Cross the stile then bear left following the wall for 100m until you reach another wall. Turn right along this for 30m to reach another stile and gate.

From the stile head out along the main track over a stream and up to a hole in a wall 300m away. From here carry straight on for 200m before dropping down to the right past some vague workings to reach a gate and stile at GR 750 154.

From here follow the wet and rough track downhill for 1km until you reach some old tied-up gates just above some sheep pens. Go through the gates (being careful to tie them up again). Then pass through the pens, over a ford and along the track beyond for 1km to reach the A487. Join this busy road, turning right up and over the col into the Tal-y-llyn valley beyond. As you begin to freewheel there is a lay-by on the right and 100m beyond this is a gate on the right. Turn right here onto the old road (bridleway) and drop roughly down this towards Cwmrhwyddfor farm. At the end of the track turn left then right back onto the A487. Continue as far as the Tal-y-llyn turning where you bear right.

After 700m the road turns 90 degrees left but you go straight on along a minor road at GR 727 110. Ford a wide ford(!) then follow the road around the lake side for 2.5km. You will then pass a house on the right at the end of the lake and shortly afterwards turn right along a signposted(!) bridleway. You are now crossing the famous Tal-y-llyn bar (the giant landslip which caused the lake and sends geography teachers into fits of gesticulation and ecstasy!). Soon you rejoin the road and coast down the far side of the bar for 2km. Where the main road goes left over a bridge, you should bear right along the northern river bank.

Follow this for 2km to a T-junction. Turn right and soon you will drop pleasantly into the Dysynni valley and a junction. If you still have time and energy, a pleasant diversion is to turn right to visit Castell y Bere at GR 669 086 1km away. This ruined castle is steeped in Welsh history and provides a fine viewpoint.

From the junction at GR 663 080, the route home lies to the left as the road winds easily through the valley towards Craig yr Aderyn (Bird's Rock), the farthest inland nesting site of cormorants in the country. Where the road forks at GR 643 072, take the right fork and cross the valley to rejoin the route out of Llanegryn at Bryn-gwyn some 4km away. From here retrace your steps to the carpark.

Cadair Idris from Barmouth Slabs

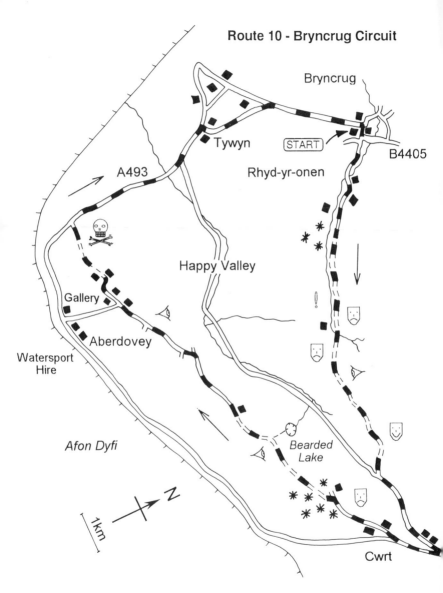

Route 10 - Bryncrug Circuit

Bryncrug

Tywyn

START

B4405

A493

Rhyd-yr-onen

Happy Valley

Gallery

Aberdovey

Watersport
Hire

Afon Dyfi

Bearded
Lake

Cwrt

N

1km

10. Bryncrug Circuit

Bryncrug, Rhyd-yr-onen, Nant Braich-y-Rhiw, Cwrt, Llyn Barfog (Bearded Lake), Ffridd yr Ychen, Crychnant, Cwm Safn-ast, Bryncrug.

Map = OS Landranger no. 135 Aberystwyth
Best conditions = Any but particularly nice in snow!
Length = 29km of which 14km are road
Height gain/loss = 620m
Time = 3-5 hours
Stars = **

This route starts from the village of Bryncrug on the A493 between Tywyn and Dolgellau at GR 609 028. It follows good, well-marked tracks with a large amount of rough climbing broken up throughout the route. It has a feeling of remoteness about it which is completely unfounded in fact! There are excellent views and some interesting cycling.

From the village of Bryncrug at GR 609 028, take the B4405 towards Tal-y-llyn for 200m. Where this road turns sharp left, carry straight on along the minor road towards Rhyd-Yr-Onen station. Go over a bridge and pass a phone box (pass one? I doubt if I could even swallow one!) before climbing along the narrow road. You will pass through two gates. At the second gate the road becomes a track, and from here the going gets harder. After a third gate, the track begins to give a sporting challenge and at the fourth it really throws down the gauntlet with a ford followed by a steep rough hill. At the top of the hill is the fifth gate which is some 4km from the station.

At this gate turn to the left and round the north end of Bryn Dinas. Soon you will find yourself in a fine position high above the Happy Valley, heading east. For the next 3km you will enjoy some technical and wet sections as well as a view over to the Bearded Lake. Soon you will descend steeply to a minor road where it is possible to take a short-cut home by turning right and dropping through the Happy Valley. For those who want to continue, bear left and race down the hill for 2km to the small village of Cwrt at the junction with the A493. Turn right along the A road and follow it for 1km where you turn first right up a minor road (dead-end) with the entrance to Cefn crib caravan park opposite, GR 680 994. Follow this narrow road steeply uphill until some farm buildings come into view next to the road. Turn left dropping away from the road down a track towards a forest 330m away.

Pass through the forest for 200m and continue up the steep track beyond. Follow the track as it then levels out and gives some wonderful views over the Dyfi estuary. 1.45km from the road you will reach an obvious junction just before a gate and stile on a hill. Leave the bikes here (**the next section is footpath only**) and follow the track on your right on foot to the Bearded Lake which you will reach after 330m. From here you can look back over the first few kilometres of the route.

Return to your bikes and continue along your original route through the gate. The grassy track leads on for 1km to a farm. Just beyond this is a minor road which you follow. Once again you will be in a fine position high above Happy Valley with views on a clear day over to the Lleyn Peninsular and Snowdonia. Eventually, you will pass some chalets on the right. Just where the road bends sharply to the left, dropping to the picturesque village of Aberdovey, there is an access road to the chalets on the right. Here you should go straight on along a good track leading to a farm 500m away. Go through the farm carefully following the blue arrows of the bridleway and trying not to disturb the farm residents. Once through the farm keep to the edge of the hedge and fence still following the blue arrows until you reach the head of a track 900m from the farm.

Drop down the steep, stony track past a graveyard and then join the A493. Turn to the right along the busy road which you follow for 3.2km. Turn second right along a narrow lane past the Marconi Cottages. Follow this due north for around 1.5km to rejoin the A493 on the far side of Tywyn. Turn right and soon you will have returned to Bryncrug.

Looking back down Rhyd-yr-onen

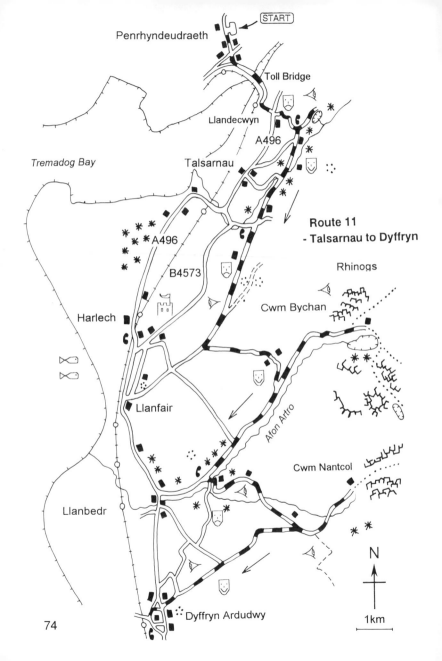

START

Penrhyndeudraeth

Toll Bridge

Llandecwyn

A496

Tremadog Bay

Talsarnau

**Route 11
- Talsarnau to Dyffryn**

A496

Rhinogs

B4573

Cwm Bychan

Harlech

Llanfair

Afon Artro

Cwm Nantcol

Llanbedr

Dyffryn Ardudwy

N

74

1km

RHINOGAU AREA

11. Talsarnau to Dyffryn

Penrhyndeudraeth, Llandecwyn (BR), Gelli Grin, Coed Felinrhyd, Llyn Tecwyn Uchaf, Llandecwyn, Llyn Tecwyn Isaf, Eisingrug, Fonlief Hir, Gerddi Bluog, Cwm Bychan, Pen-y-bont, Gelli Bant, Coed Ystumgwern, Dyffryn Ardudwy (BR).

Map = OS no. 124 Dolgellau
Best conditions = Evening for the sunset
Length = 35km entirely on narrow country lanes
Height gain = 700m.
Time = 2 4 hours
Stars = **

This route starts from Penrhyndeudraeth station at GR 612 388 on the Cambrian coastline and is a linear route joined by a short rail journey. It is entirely confined to narrow country lanes which run through remote and beautiful scenery. There are several long hills in both directions and lakes, rivers, woods etc. It is possible to park in Penrhyndeudraeth or Dyffryn Ardudwy depending at which end you start from.

From Penrhyndeudraeth station at GR 612 388 turn right following the toll road over the toll bridge and Avon Dwyryd. Then head up the hill to a staggered + junction at approximately 2km. Go straight over and climb steeply out of the village up a winding hill. Drop quickly down the far side for a short way only to be faced with another steep climb to a junction at a phone box at 3.12km. Turn left to reach a junction next to Llyn Tecwyn Isaf at 3.38km. Pause to admire the view for a while then return to the telephone box and take the only option that you have not yet tried.

Before you do this you may wish to fork left at 3.38km, climbing up another steep hill to reach a chapel with brilliant views over the Dwyryd Estuary, Portmeirion and Snowdonia. From here reverse your steps to the phone box at the junction and rejoin the route.

Follow the road up and then down again ignoring right turns at 3.67km and 4.92km. Head through the quiet valley and over a humpback bridge before climbing up a steep hill passing Maes y Neuadd Hotel. Ignore a dead-end road to the left at 6.3km and then turn left at 6.5km up a road signposted to Llanfair (just before a telephone box). Climb steeply up to top out at the third gate at 8.9km.

At this point you may wish to walk along the next track on the left for a few hundred yards to visit several standing stones and cairn circles. **NB! This small detour is on a footpath, so please leave your bikes behind.**

Drop down the hill to 10.38km where a road leads off to the left, signposted Cwm Bychan. Follow this road in good style with an excellent series of hairpins which drop you down the hillside through a farm at Gerddi Bluog which used to be a Youth Hostel. Keep winding down, having a great time, to a T-junction at 13.98km. You are now in the delightful Cwm Bychan valley. Turn left and follow the road up to the head of the lake at 16.65km. The view from here is excellent but it is worthwhile continuing as far as the campsite at 17.57km in order to fully appreciate the ruggedness of the Rhynog mountain range. If you are lucky you may see some wild mountain goats on this section of road.

From the campsite you must retrace your steps as far as the last T-junction which you pass at 21.49km. Keep straight on here, dropping down the valley until it is possible to turn left over a bridge at 25.03km and GR 600 273. Cross the bridge and then take the first left at 25.13km and climb the steep road. At 25.7km it is worth looking over the edge of the steep gorge which you are passing and then stopping at the reservoir at 25.91km.

Keep climbing up this road until you reach a dead-end road sign next to a right-hand turn at 29.32km. Take the right-hand turn and follow this with excellent views to a T-junction at 32.21km. Turn right and fly down the road to Dyffryn Ardudwy - try not to get booked for speeding! At 34.5km you reach a T-junction with the main coast road. Go straight over the road and down the lane opposite to a T-junction where you turn left at 34.75km. Follow this to yet another T-junction where you turn right at 35.1km and follow this to the railway station at 35.21km. Now all you have to do is catch a train back to Penrhyndeudraeth. It is worth checking prior to doing the route that you are able to get your bike on the train as this can sometimes be a problem.

Route 12 - Trawsfynydd

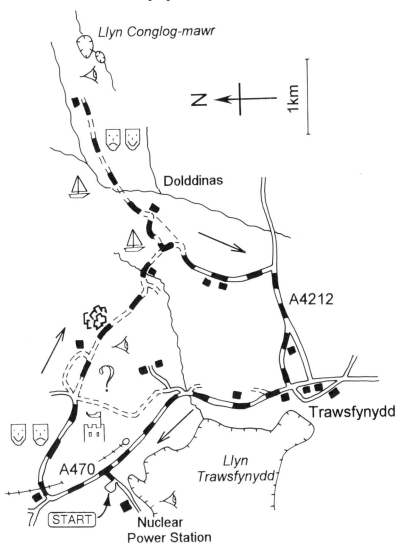

Llyn Conglog-mawr

N

1km

Dolddinas

A4212

Trawsfynydd

Llyn Trawsfynydd

A470

START

Nuclear Power Station

12. Trawsfynydd

Trawsfynydd Nuclear Power station, Llyn yr Oerfel, Dolddinas, Llyn
Conglog Mawr, Dolddinas, Trawsfynydd, Castell Tomen-y-mur,
Trawsfynydd Nuclear Power Station.

Map = OS no. 124 Dolgellau
Best conditions = Whilst the reactors are shut down!
Length = 17km of which 9km are on roads
Height gain = 500m
Time = 2-3 hours

**This difficult route starts from the carpark at GR 696 384 inside
the grounds of the nuclear power station. There is some hard
riding, tricky navigation and a short section of fast A-road. On
the other hand there are several good views and some historical
interest as well as one nice downhill section. Not a classic but
not without value. You may wish to visit the now de-
commissioned power station and the nature trail next to the
lake.**

From the round carpark at GR 696 384 turn left and go up to the
power station gates before turning left again along the A470. Follow
this to 1.25km (the pavement may feel safer!) where you turn right
passing under a railway bridge and climbing up a long steepish hill.
At 2.94km the road bears sharp left to a TV mast and a track goes
straight on past a sign which reads "All dogs must be on a leash".
Follow this good track passing Llyn yr Oerfel on your left. Continue
past some old mine workings eventually to reach the end of the good
track at 4.35km just to the right of a small quarry.

Follow a grassy track in the same direction to 4.44km. Take the lower right fork which leads you over and down to a better track at some sheepfolds and a ruin at 5.16km and GR 725 379. Turn left crossing the small ford before bearing right off the track and along the edge of a wall. Carry here for 100m until the ground levels off and the track gradually improves as it follows the wall under the electricity pylons at 5.45km. Turn left along a better track at 5.88km. Pass the ruins at Dolddinas before fording Afon Llafar at 6.45km. You have by now passed several Roman practice works though quite what they were practising for I do not know!

Climb the long and loose hill with much energy consumption. Pass a track to some old mine workings before reaching the end of the track at 7.5km. Though the bridleway continues for a few metres beyond this, it fails to reach Llyn Conglog-mawr by some distance. So, after a short rest and a glance at the moors, the return leg beckons.

Drop quickly down the technical track and over the ford. From here, follow the track generally downhill with some fine views until you reach the head of a road at 10.68km. Keep going until you reach the A4212 at 11.54km and GR 725 360. Turn right along this then first right at 12.6km. Drop through a village and along a high-walled road to reach the A470 at 13.59km. Turn right along this and then keep going for 3.5km to return to the carpark and your car.

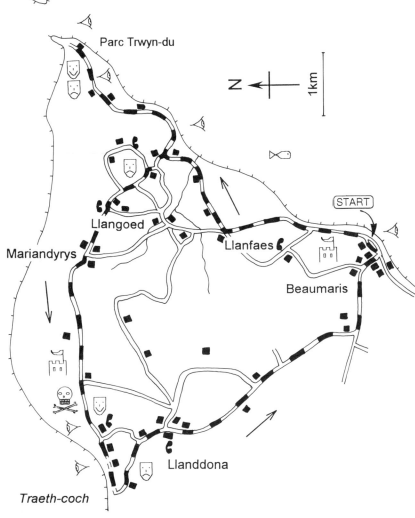

Ynys Seiriol
(Puffin Island)

Route 13 - Beaumaris

Parc Trwyn-du

N ← | 1km

START

Llangoed

Llanfaes

Beaumaris

Mariandyrys

Llanddona

Traeth-coch

82

ANGLESEY

13. Beaumaris

Beaumaris, Penmon, Parc Trwyn-du, Penmon, Mariandyrys, Traeth-coch, Llanddona, Beaumaris.

Map = OS no. 115 Snowdon
Best conditions = When the sea is rough
Length = 26.5km entirely on road (almost)
Height gain = 400m
Time = 1.5 - 3 hours
Stars = *

This road-bound route starts from the large seafront carpark at GR 606 759 in Beaumaris on Ynys Mon (Anglesey). It is a pleasant introduction to cycling on the quiet roads of the island and is ideal for families, those who do not want to go off road and for bad weather days. As the island is low it tends to miss much of the weather and consequently when the mountains of Snowdonia are shrouded in cloud, it can often be fine on the far side of the Menai Strait. The route offers superb sea views and a unique view back to Snowdonia as well as many historic diversions. The riding and navigation are straightforward and there is only one real hill to speak of.

From the seafront carpark at GR 606 759 in Beaumaris turn right then right again in front of the Castle and cycle gently north out of town. Climb easily to 2.93km where you turn right at a crossroads towards Penmon.

This road winds along the coast passing some pleasant shingle beaches with good views into Snowdonia. Ignore a road to the left at GR 622 798, following the main road sharply right. At 7km you pass the ancient monument of Penmon Priory and Dovecote from circa 16th century in the minute village of Penmon. Continue past the priory up a short steep hill before drifting quickly down to Parc Trwyn-du and its excellent view of Ynys Seiriol (Priestholm or Puffin Island) and the rocky coast to the west. There are toilets and a café here so it makes an excellent picnic spot.

When you are rested, turn through 180 degrees and retrace your steps past the priory and beaches to 11.48km. Here you can take the first road on the right which means going straight on where the main road goes sharp left just after a bus shelter.

Follow this narrow road as it zigzags uphill quite steeply for 1km before levelling off for just under 1km. At the end of the level section the road will begin to drop and you will pass two dead-end roads on the right, before bearing left and dropping quickly towards some houses. As the road steepens, turn right at 13.05km down a road with an "Unsuitable for long vehicles" sign. Follow this down then up to a steep T-junction in Mariandyrys at 13.93km. Turn right here up the hill.

After a short climb the going eases. At 16km you pass a turning on the right to Bwrdd Arthur hill fort which you may wish to visit. **NB! Please note that the tracks leading to the fort are solely footpaths, so leave your bikes behind!** At 16.47km you will have come round a sharp left turn and should now turn right in front of the TV mast. This road begins to drop very quickly towards Traeth-coch but great care should be taken as the road is steep, narrow and has poor visibility.

At 17.62km you reach a church where you turn right between it and the telephone box before dropping to Traeth-coch (Red Wharf bay). Cycle along the rough beach track (marked on the OS as a footpath, but is in fact a bridleway, in the process of being upgraded to an unclassified minor road) for 1km until it becomes a road again and leads you away from the beach. This is the hill of the route so set to and get it over with but remember to look back before the top

Penmon lighthouse with Ynys Seiriol behind

to admire the view (that's my excuse and I'm sticking to it!).

At 19.88km you reach a T-junction with the worst of the hill behind you. Turn right climbing into Llanddona where you turn right again at a T-junction next to the Owain Glyndwr Pub - which may prove too much for some! Follow the road out of the village passing a monument and dropping quickly to a T-junction at 24.57km. Turn left and drop very quickly towards Beaumaris.

Reach a T-junction with the B5109 at 26.05km. Turn left then first right, go straight over the seafront road and reach the carpark at 26.4km. Time for a paddle in the sea!

Route 14 - Cefn Coch

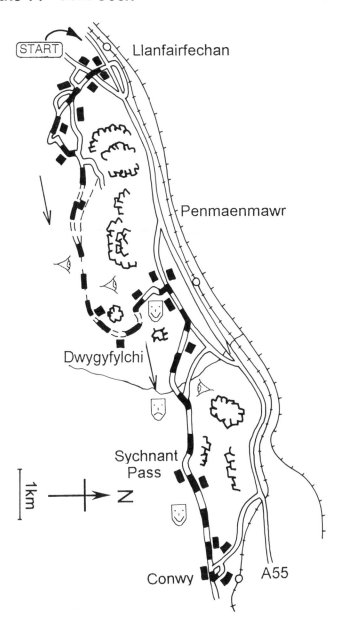

START

Llanfairfechan

Penmaenmawr

Dwygyfylchi

Sychnant
Pass

1km

N

Conwy

A55

CARNEDDAU AREA

14. Cefn Côch

Llanfairfechan, Cefn Côch, Bryn Derwydd, Dwygyfylchi, Sychnant Pass, Conwy.

Map = OS no. 115 Snowdon
Best conditions = Evening for the sunset
Length = 16km of which 11km are on minor roads
Height gain = 500m
Time = 1.5-3 hours
Stars = *

This short route follows an excellent RUPP and bridleway over Cefn Côch on the northern flanks of the Carneddau range. It is set in a fine position between the mountains and the sea and as a result suffers from an overdose of good views. There are two big hills to contend with but otherwise the going is good. A short train journey completes the trip - though it is possible to cycle back along the A55 but this is not recommended. Parts of this route are to be included in a new walking guide and may therefore see an increase in use - please give way to walkers.

From the railway station in Llanfairfechan at GR 677 751, head along the road past the bowling club etc. to reach a T-junction after 170m or so. Turn right under the railway (there is a carpark to the left).

Climb to a crossroads at some traffic lights at 0.75km. Go straight over the lights then turn first left just after the fire station up "Valley Road" at 1.1km.

Continue climbing gently to 1.27km where you turn left up "Mount Road" and prepare for a long steep hill. Fight your way up for 1.5km until at 2.66km you reach a point where you can actually roll forward unaided. You will come across four concrete bollards opposite two left turns at GR 695 746. Take the second left turn and **not** the Plas Heulog option.

This road leads you up to 3.1km. Continue straight on where the road turns sharp left to Penmaenmawr quarries. Go through a gate which leads to a farm at 3.27km. This is a working farm and home to a family so please **walk quietly** through the farmyard until you leave the farm at a gate directly in front of the farmhouse.

Climb the grassy track beyond until you reach two gates at 3.82km. Take the left-hand gate and continue to the next gate at 4.11km. At this point the view over to Ynys Mon (Anglesey) is quite spectacular. Go through the gate and follow the vaguer track beyond through open country (Cefn Côch) to 4.6km. Pass through several stone circles, known as the Druid Circles.

Keep going through the col, with good views at 5.3km. Stay on the more obvious left-hand track which drops towards a wall and passes under some power cables. This track leads you back up and then to the left of a small building before reaching a gate above a house at 6.48km and GR 730 749.

Go through the gate and pass in front of the house (Bryn Derwydd) keeping to the track until another joins it from the right at 7.44km. Continue in your general direction and drop down a very steep hill as far as some huge stone gateposts at 7.94km.

Note: please moderate your speed if there are walkers on the track.

In front of the gateposts follow the road round to the left and quickly down (beware blind bends) to a T-junction at 9.23km.

Turn right and follow this to another T-junction near a chapel at 9.57km. Turn right again and cycle pleasantly along to the bottom of the Sychnant Pass. Gird your loins and go for it - middle chainring is possible but not easy. Climb over the top and then drop happily down the far side speeding along the wide, well-surfaced road. Drop through the old town wall and into the centre of Conwy at 16km. A pleasant few hours can be lost looking around the castle and the harbour etc. in Conwy.

From here it is best to catch a train back to Llanfairfechan as the A55 coast road is very busy and not a place for cyclists unless you enjoy sucking in fumes!

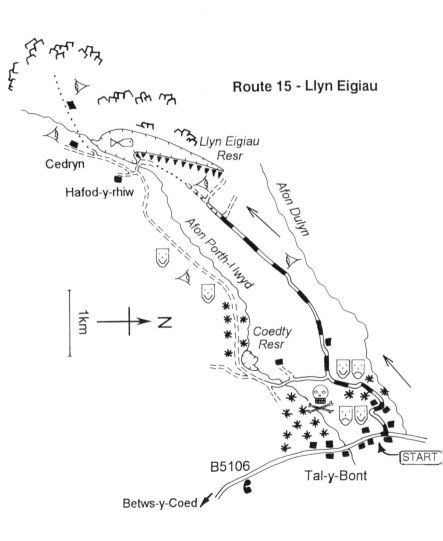

Route 15 - Llyn Eigiau

Llyn Eigiau Resr

Afon Dulyn

Cedryn

Hafod-y-rhiw

Afon Porth-Llwyd

1km

N

Coedty Resr

B5106

Tal-y-Bont

START

Betws-y-Coed

15. Llyn Eigiau

Tal-y-Bont, Llyn Eigiau Reservoir, Hafod-y-rhiw, Coedty Reservoir,
Tal-y-Bont.

Map = OS no. 115 Snowdon
Best Conditions = Any
Length = 11km of which all are on very minor roads
Height gain = 350m
Time = 1-2 hours
Stars = **

**This surprising and beautiful route starts from the village of
Tal-y-Bont in a small lay-by opposite the Post Office at GR 767
686, though there is plenty of roadside parking in the village. It
climbs steeply up a minor road to reach Llyn Eigiau Reservoir
with its stunning views into Cwm Eigiau and the Carneddau.
The road is extremely quiet and the surfaces in general are good
though there is one desperate hill at the start.**

From the small lay-by on the road between the Post Office and Tal-y-
Bont Garage in the village of Tal-y-Bont at GR 767 686, turn towards
Conwy and cycle north on the B5106. After 200m turn first left up a
narrow lane between some renovated houses (Yr Hen Felin). There
are occasional nice views down the Conwy valley but you may be
too preoccupied to notice. Climb gently to begin with between high
hedges as the road zigzags upwards, getting steeper and steeper
until it has you reaching for the granny gears and wishing that you
had warmed up and stretched before you started.

After 1km of very steep pain the road levels off. At 2.24km you
reach a fork in the road at GR 757 679 where you bear right - which

means more or less straight on. 100m beyond this go through a gate and then coast down to a farm. Pass this, climbing through trees until you reach the brow of the hill in a superb position looking into the Carneddau and Cwm Eigiau. Follow the easy road towards the beautiful vista ahead. At 5.7km you reach the end of the road at a small Snowdonia National Park carpark at GR 731 662.

The dam wall in front of you collapsed in November 1925 causing loss of life in Dolgarrog and widespread flooding. There are several beautiful walks from this carpark **but no cycling** so about face and head back down the way you came.

Note: the hill is extremely fast and steep with no room for bike versus car encounters - so beware. Drop down (marvelling at how steep it is and at the fact that you actually cycled up it) avoiding a serious crash into a wall or hedge until you reach the bottom of the hill at a T-junction. Turn right returning to your car at 10.4km. Nice work!

Crossing the dike en route to Llyn Cowlyd, route 16 Llyn Cowlyd to Llyn Geirionydd

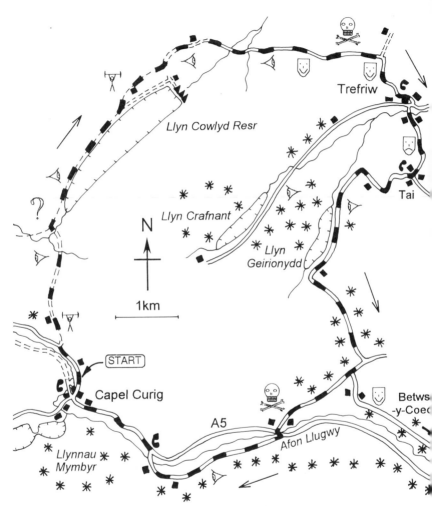

Llyn Cowlyd Resr

Trefriw

Tai

Llyn Crafnant

N

Llyn
Geirionydd

1km

START

Capel Curig

A5

Betws
-y-Coed

Afon Llugwy

Llynnau
Mymbyr

Route 16 - Llyn Cowlyd to Llyn Geirionydd

16. Llyn Cowlyd to Llyn Geirionydd

Capel Curig, Helyg, Tal-y-braich, Pont y Bedol, Bwlch Cowlyd, Llyn Cowlyd, Garreg-wen, Cefn Cyfarwydd, Trefriw, Llanrhychwyn, Llyn Geirionydd, Ty-hyll, Pont Cyfyng, Capel Curig.

Map = OS no. 115 Snowdon or Outdoor Leisure 16 Snowdonia Conwy Valley area
Best conditions = After several days of hard frost
Length = 30km of which 19km are on minor roads
Height gain = 600m
Time = 2.5 - 5 hours
Stars = **

This tough route starts from the new Snowdonia National Park carpark beyond Joe Brown's outdoor shop in Capel Curig at GR 720 582. It uses stony tracks, grassy tracks, narrow paths and minor roads in the hills above Betws-y-Coed. It has several large, steep climbs and offers some excellent views not normally seen. Alternative parking and start points can be found in the carparks in the Ogwen Valley to the north-west. Care must be taken not to cause damage on the first few kilometres especially after prolonged rain when the ground may be waterlogged.

From the carpark behind Joe Brown's shop in Capel Curig at GR 720 582 turn left dropping past the shop. Turn left onto the A5 towards Bangor after 170m. Follow the A5 to 1.05km and GR 718 589 where you turn right through a kissing gate and 5-bar gate beneath a green sign. Let a significant amount of air out of your back tyre before climbing gently up the grassy path under the power cables. If you find your wheel spinning, get off and push to avoid damage to the path. Eventually you are forced to carry anyway up a short rocky step at 1.41km. Above the step, head over to the farm, crossing a track at 1.55km before heading round the back of the farm.

This wet and muddy track leads you up to a gate and stile at 1.91km. Go over the stile then bear right up the grassy track beyond following it across the moor.

This section is liable to damage when wet so please take care by walking the boggy sections and not forcing the route. At 3.04km you reach a bridge over a dike. Beyond this bear left along the fence to reach a wooden bridge at 3.41km and GR 716 609. From the bridge bear right and follow the track with some boggy bits to the Llyn Cowlyd Reservoir with more excellent views. Follow the bridleway round the north-west edge of the lake watching out for a short section where the track has eroded into the lake leaving a steep and dangerous drop.

Follow the main track up a short steep hill passing some large boulders at 5.7km. A little beyond these - at 5.96km - bear left up a vague, grassy track 50m or so before a wall. Join the wall where it bends and follow it up to a ruined farm at 6.2km. You will probably have to carry for 100m. Pass behind the farm then drop through some sheep-pens to rejoin the track/path at the far side of the farm. Follow the grassy path up to a stile at 6.5km, then continue through heather until you join a larger track close to a small hut at 6.93km. Turn right dropping for a few metres to take the first left turn at 9.03km.

Drop to Garreg-wen farm (deserted) at 10.1km. Just beyond the farm you pass under the ugly pipeline that runs from the reservoir.

Just beyond the pipeline bear right and drop to the metalled road. From here climb steeply up the road to reach the top of the hill after a hard fight at 12.09km (more excellent views). You now drop down towards the valley, heading due east. This is great fun with several very steep hairpins and fast sections - but beware, it is easy to go too fast on this section and wipe out in a serious way. At 15.04km you will reach a T-junction in upper Trefriw. Turn right and then left after 120m.

Follow this road out of the village and up an extremely steep hill that goes on for ever until you arrive half-dead (at least) at a + junction at 16.64km. Turn right and follow this road gently round to pass the

Llyn Geirionydd on a peaceful afternoon

picturesque Llyn Geirionydd. Just past the southern end of the lake, follow the road sharp left and climb to a T-junction at 22.14km. Turn right and follow this road down to the A5 at 24.34km. The Ugly House (Ty-hyll) is to your right at this point and is worth a visit.

The Ty-hyll was built in 1475 by two outlaw brothers. If you could assemble a rough house overnight and have smoke coming from its chimney by dawn you could then claim the land it was built on and any that was within an axe's throw of the building. This basic house is the result of that tradition.

Turn left onto the A5 and cross the bridge. Turn immediately right down a minor road which you follow pleasantly to Pont Cyfyng and the A5 at 27.31km. Turn left and follow the A5 back to Capel Curig and the start of the route at 29.31km.

Route 17 - Llyn Crafnant

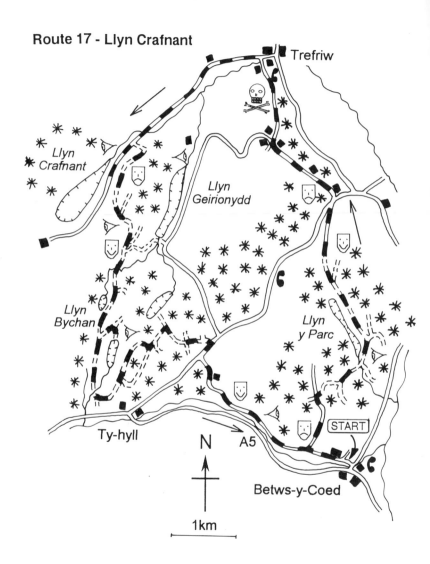

Trefriw

Llyn Crafnant

Llyn Geirionydd

Llyn Bychan

Llyn y Parc

START

Ty-hyll

N

A5

Betws-y-Coed

1km

BETWS-Y-COED AREA

17. Llyn Crafnant

Betws-y-Coed, Pen-yr-allt, Llyn y Parc, Parc lead mine, Tai, Trefriw, Llyn Crafnant, Mynydd Deulyn, Llyn Geirionydd, Ty'n-y-mynydd, Pencraig, Betws-y-Coed.

Map = OS no. 115 Snowdon or Outdoor Leisure 16 Snowdownia Conwy Valley
Best conditions = Any
Length = 25.5km of which 12km are on country lanes
Height Gain = 650m
Time = 2-4 hours
Stars = **

This route starts from the carpark over the bridge from the Climber and Rambler outdoor shop in Betws-y-Coed at GR 791 567. It uses minor roads and forest tracks to visit numerous lakes and to take in one of the best views in the country i.e. that of the Llyn Crafnant and the mountains around it.

From the carpark opposite the Climber and Rambler outdoor shop in Betws-y-Coed at GR 791 567 continue west along the minor road that leads into the forest. After 770m, turn right up a narrow road which climbs ridiculously steeply until you have come a total of 1.95km. Having gone round the back of Pen-yr-allt farm you should take the next track on the right into the forest.

Follow this track round to a road triangle at 2.54km. Turn left and follow the main track up and then down to the southern end of Llyn y Parc at 3.1km. Bear left and follow the eastern edge of the lake. Bear left at a junction at 3.52km. At 4.63km you can turn left down a narrower track which quickly drops to become metalled as it passes the lead mines. At 5.94km you will reach a minor road at a T-junction. Turn right then first left and climb a series of short steep hills to 7.82km. Here you turn right at a + junction near a telephone box in the tiny hamlet of Tai.

Follow this narrow road very quickly down to Trefriw but be aware of a very sharp left turn at the bottom of the hill. Keep on this road until it brings you up to a T-junction at 9.3km. Turn left and follow this road up through delightful woods until you suddenly arrive at the monument at the north-eastern end of Llyn Crafnant at 12.59km. Get out your camera and fire away!

When you have had your fill of the view, turn round and head back down the road as far as the carpark at 12.97km. Turn right up a forest road, through a gate and then bear sharp right at some low crags/quarries. **Note: this area is a favourite with walkers and families of unsuspecting tourists so please moderate your speed on the way down the far side**.

This track leads you above the lake in a beautiful situation and over Mynydd Deulyn with several excellent viewpoints. Ignore a left T-junction at 14.79km and then drop to some sharp bends where you bear right at 15.51km. Drop through graceful bends to 14.64km where you take the first right turn through a gate and out of the forest.

Climb gently back into the forest at a gate. Turn right at a T-junction at 16.4km passing to the east of Llyn Bychan. Turn first left at 17.18km then first right 220m beyond which leads you down to the picturesque Llyn Goddionduon at 17.56km. Return to the main track at GR 751 588. Continue quickly down the hill ignoring any turnings to either side until you reach an obvious fork in the track at 19.6km. The right fork drops through a recently cleared area and the left fork (which you take) climbs through the trees.

Climb to a T-junction at 20.8km. Turn right going straight over the next T-junction as you leave the main forest and drop to reach a road at 21.65km. Turn right coasting to the first left turn at 21.9km. Drop steeply down from this road with several sharp bends passing Pencraig farm and then undulating through the picturesque forest until you return to the carpark at 25.3km. Cafés and cake shops over the bridge!

Forest track above Llyn y Parc, route 18 Llyn y Parc

Route 18 - Llyn y Parc

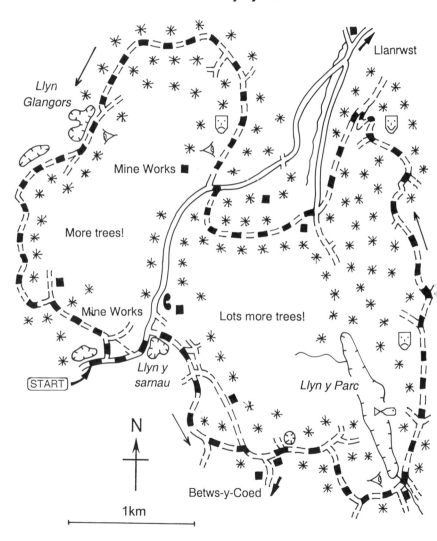

Llanrwst

Llyn Glangors

Mine Works ■

More trees!

Mine Works

Lots more trees!

Llyn y sarnau

Llyn y Parc

START

N

Betws-y-Coed

1km

18. Llyn y Parc

Llyn y Sarnau, Llyn y Parc, Pen-y-parc, Hafno Lead Mine, Castell y Gwynt, Llyn y Sarnau.

Map = OS no. 115 Snowdon
Best conditions = Any
Length = 12.5km of which 800m are on minor roads
Height gain = 250m.
Time = 1 hour plus
Stars = *

This short forest route starts from a roadside carpark at GR 773 588 and stays almost entirely on forest tracks. There are no difficult hills to climb and the views are good with some historical interest along the way. This makes it a good route for families.

From the roadside lay-by/carpark at GR 773 588 turn right up the hill and coast along to Llyn y Sarnau. At the end of the lake turn right at 0.77km onto a forest track. Fork right at 0.92km and follow this road along the edge of a field, dropping down to a fork at 1.64km. Bear left at the fork, climbing for a short while before dropping past a pool at 2.27km. Follow the main track round to the right at 2.56 km. This track leads you to a T-junction at 3km, where you turn left to arrive at the southern end of Llyn y Parc at 3.34km. This spot makes a nice picnic site.

Continue along the track beside the lake until you reach a large three-way junction at 3.62km and GR 795 588. Turn off the main track and climb steeply up the middle track. This leads you over Pen-y-parc before descending to 5.54km. Turn sharp right on the outside of a bend and drop quickly to a sharp left turn at 6.15km. Follow this in a nice position with good views. Go straight over a road at 6.8km before climbing up towards Hafno Lead Mines. You will reach a minor road at 7.81km. Turn left then first right in front of the newly restored mine workings (worth a quick visit) and climb a long hill to take the second right at 8.9km.

Climb past Castell y Gwynt and a small fenced-off lake at 10.12km just before bearing right at a T-junction at 10.15km. Follow this track with some good views to a right turn at the next T-junction at 11.51km. Fork right at 11.88km and then turn right onto the road at 12.06km returning to the start point at 12.3km.

Cycling past the restored tin mines

Route 19 - Llyn Elsi Reservoir

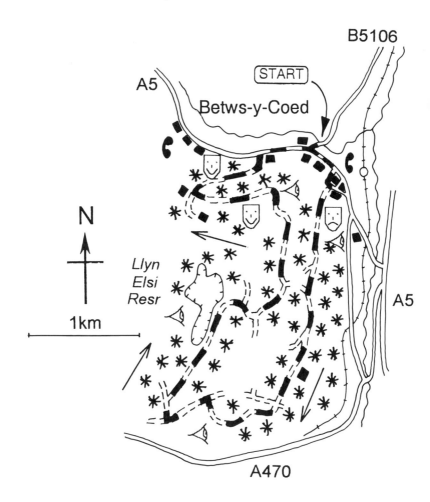

19. Llyn Elsi Reservoir

Betws-y-Coed, Coed-y-celyn, Llyn Elsi, Betws-y-Coed.

Map = OS no. 115 Snowdon
Best conditions = Any
Length = 10km of which 1km is on road
Height gain = 250m
Time = 1-2 hours
Stars = **

**This short forest route starts from the small carpark at GR 791
567 though there is plenty of alternative parking in the village. It
stays mainly on forest roads, some of which are quite rough.
There is one hard climb at the beginning and a good descent at
the end with the in-between bits pretty much straightforward.
There are some excellent views particularly at Llyn Elsi which
is a fine picnic spot.**

From the small carpark at GR 791 567 in Betws-y-Coed (just over
the bridge from the Climber and Rambler) cross the bridge and turn
left at the T-junction in front of the shop. Wind your way slowly through
the village, taking care for tourists. At 0.4km you can turn first right in
front of a large church. Climb a short hill until it bends to the left. At
this point you go straight on through a forest barrier and onto a well-
made but steep forest road.

Climb very steeply through the trees. At 1.2km the track levels off
somewhat and there is a viewpoint sign on the left. **Walk** down the

path to the viewpoint which you reach after 100m - you will probably be glad of the rest! Having recovered and returned to your bikes, continue in the same direction up the now gentler hill passing a minor left turn at 1.65km to reach a T-junction at 1.87km.

Turn left following the undulating track to 2.38km where you fork left over the brow of a hill. Keep undulating as you pass a lonely house in a clearing on the left at Coed-y-celyn and continue down to a T-junction at 3.28km. This junction is in fact a + junction and you go straight over following the track round to the right high above the valley floor with wide views. Soon you turn back into the forest to reach a T-junction at 4.1km.

Turn left uphill to 4.51km. Turn right up a winding hill to turn right again at 4.92km through a barrier. Climb until you come out at a viewpoint at the southern end of Llyn Elsi Reservoir at 5.65km. Continue along the edge of the lake with beautiful views until the road turns away from the lake and drops to a T-junction at 6.19km. Turn right then first left at 6.36km dropping quickly to 6.81km. Bear left here before climbing up and over a short hill with a brief, rough section and a fine viewpoint.

Note: the next section is quick and narrow so please restrict your speed and watch out for walkers.

Continue down the hill through a turning circle which appears to be a dead-end but is not, until the track doubles back on itself at 8.7km. Drop quickly to reach the road at 9.48km. Turn right into Betws-y-Coed then left over the bridge at 9.9km to return to the carpark at 10km.

Moel Siabod from the forest around Betws-y-Coed

Route 20 - Circuit of Moel Siabod

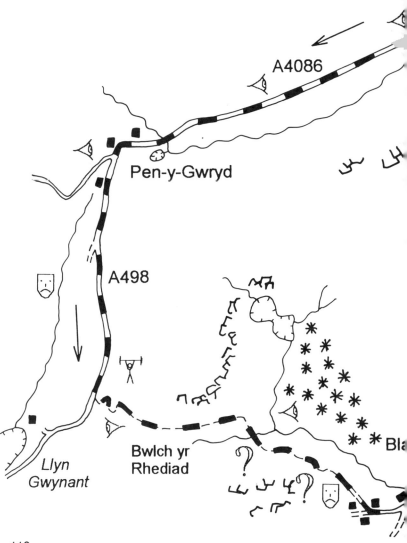

A4086

Pen-y-Gwryd

A498

Bwlch yr
Rhediad

*Llyn
Gwynant*

Bla

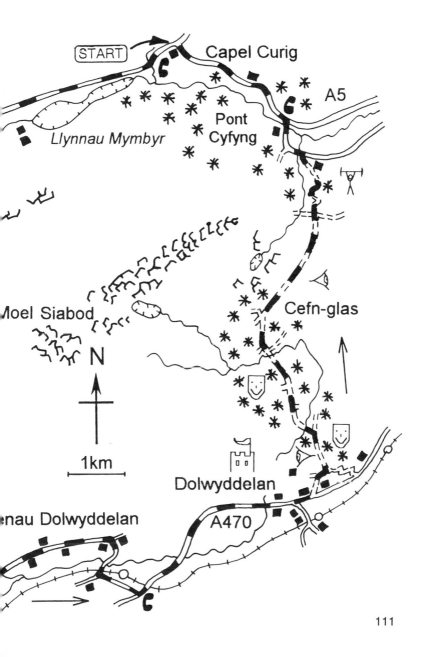

111

SNOWDON AREA

20. Circuit of Moel Siabod

Capel Curig, Pen-y-Gwryd, Bwlch-y-Rhediad, Coed Mawr, Dolwyddelan, Cefn-glas, Pont Cyfyng, Capel Curig.

Map = OS no. 115 Snowdon
Best conditions = After several hard frosts. Should be avoided in wet weather
Length = 29km of which 20km are on road
Height gain = 600m
Time = 2.5 - 5 hours
Stars = **

This tough route starts from the carpark beyond Joe Brown's Outdoor Shop in Capel Curig at GR 720 582. Some of the going is hard on wet and grassy tracks with one long carry up onto the Moelwyns. Not a route for the unfit or those who want to race but an excellent expedition for those who enjoy the mountains. You will be some distance from help at times so this route should not be attempted by those inexperienced in the mountains.

From the carpark behind Joe Brown's shop at GR 720 582, drop to the road and turn right towards Plas y Brenin and Beddgelert. Follow the A4086 past Llynnau Mymbyr and through Dyffryn Mymbyr in a fine position beneath the towering Glyders until you pass the Pen-y-Gwryd Hotel and the Llanberis Pass turning. From here, follow the A498 south into the Gwynant valley. This road remains fairly level and offers good views of the valley and Snowdon. At 10.25km or GR 657 526 there is a footpath sign (it is in fact a bridleway) on the left next to a gate and new stile.

Go over the stile then follow the bridleway as it winds up through the trees. There is a couple of short rideable sections but you will mostly have to carry until you come out above the trees at an excellent viewpoint on a rocky bluff. Keep carrying up past a small ruin until you reach a wall. Go through this then follow a larger wall across the hillside until you can go through a gap in the wall at 11.12km and onto an obvious wide, grassy track beyond at GR 662 524.

Get back on your bike and fight your way up the rough steep track to Bwlch-y-Rhediad. Go round a gate in an overgrown wall at 11.76km and look out over the Moelwyns. Follow the rough and wet track round the hillside with not inconsiderable effort. After a level section you reach a sheepfold/small ruin above a small wood at 12.69km and GR 676 525.

Go round the ruin then drop to the right keeping 50-100m left of the wood following a dry (most of the time) stream-bed. The track will slowly bear left and you should follow it down to a small footbridge which you cross at 13.06km. **Note: the next section may appear different in the future as the track is being extended towards the footbridge from Coed Mawr Farm.**

Once over the bridge go directly up the opposite hillside bearing slightly right for 100m. Carry here until the angle eases and you reach the end of a track near some boulders/small outcrops. Follow this wet track as it winds along the hillside passing small quarries and spoil heaps to reach a gate in a dry-stone wall at 13.91km.

Go through the gate then cross the boggy bit. Carry here until it dries out and you follow the track. This is vague in parts until you reach another gate at 14.64km after a descent. Flow through the next few rough corners until you drop steeply to the back of Coed Mawr farm at 15.03km. Bear left through the farm and along the track beyond until you drop to a T-junction next to a converted chapel at 15.5km.

Turn left along the road which undulates and winds its way through the valley. It comes out on the A470 just after Pont Rufeinig station at

18.52km. Turn left along the road crossing Pont-y-Coblyn and drifting into Dolwyddelan. At 21.29km (GR 737 525) turn left opposite a footpath sign up a narrow track signposted Capel Curig between some terraced houses. Climb steeply, bearing right at 21.35km and 21.4km then following the wet track up to a T-junction at 21.62km where you turn right again to reach a forest track at 21.78km.

Turn left up the long hill until you drop out of the trees into a cleared area. Cross a small stream before climbing to a junction at 23.67km. Turn right leaving the forest at a gate and small ford along a good grassy track.

Note: this next section is frequented by walkers so restrict your speed on the descent.

This good track leads you gently upwards to a + junction at 25.21km. Go straight on and begin to descend. The track gets rougher and rougher giving good sport with the distinct possibility of wipe out! Drop through a gate and down to a road at 25.88km. Turn left here and left again at Pont Cyfyng onto the A5 at 26.81km. Follow this back to Capel Curig and the carpark behind Joe Brown's shop at 29km. The nearest café is at the road triangle 200m away - or there is always the bar at the Brenin!

Reflections, near the lowest point
of the Moel Siabod circuit

Route 21 - Cefn Glas and Sarn Helen

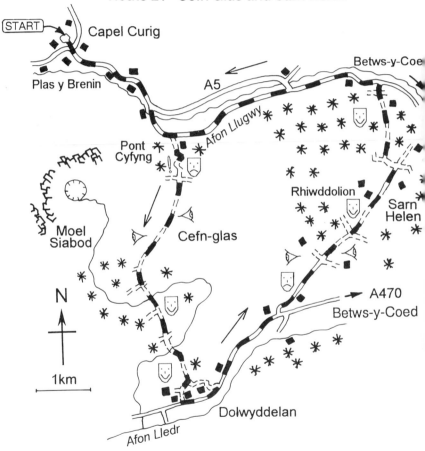

21. Cefn Glas and Sarn Helen

Capel Curig, Pont Cyfyng, Cefn Glas, Dolwyddelan, Pentre-bont, Pont-y-pant, Sarn Helen, Rhiwddolion, Craig Foris, Pont Cyfyng, Capel Curig.

Map = OS no. 115 Snowdon or Outdoor Leisure 16 Snowdonia
Conwy Valley
Best conditions = Any
Length = 24km of which 10km are on minor roads
Height gain = 300m
Time = 2 - 4 hours
Stars = **

This route starts from the new Snowdonia National Park carpark behind Joe Brown's shop in Capel Curig at GR 720 582. It uses ancient roads and forest tracks to the east of Moel Siabod to produce a charming route with surprisingly easy riding in an excellent setting. This is what mountain bikes were invented for.

From the carpark behind Joe Brown's shop in Capel Curig at GR 720 582, drop past the shop. Turn left and then right onto the A5 towards Betws-y-Coed. Follow this until you have come 1.98km where you turn right over Pont Cyfyng. Follow this road for 700m until you can turn right up a rough track at 2.55km. Pass a chapel on the left which is now a climbing club hut.

Follow the track steeply up past the chapel and through a gate after 100m (2.66km into the route). Keep on the main track as it climbs steeply and roughly up Cerrig Gwynion to 3.52km. You may have to carry over this stretch. At the + junction, go straight and follow the track along the lower flanks of Moel Siabod (excellent views) until you enter a forest. Ignore a turning to the right at 5.15km and continue to reach a junction at 5.47km.

Turn left at the junction and drop quickly down into the trees. Follow the main track over some short climbs but mostly descents. Eventually you reach a right turn just before a forest gate at 7.36km and GR 738 528. Take this right turn down the narrow track and then turn left down a steep, rocky, wet track at 7.52km. Before you do this, however, it is worth climbing **on foot** up the hill in front to look at the view over Siabod and Dolwyddelan Castle.

Follow the rocky track bearing left at 7.7km and 7.75km to reach the A470 at 7.81km. Turn left following the road pleasantly down the valley. At 10.93km you turn first left just beyond a house which has two large fir trees as gateposts. Follow this steep road up until at 11.77km you reach a + junction. Go straight on over the junction and continue on the track. You are now on the Roman road, Sarn Helen which runs down the spine of Wales and can be ridden as far away as the Vale of Neath! Follow the track until you reach a gate into the forest at 12.73km (GR 764 550).

Go into the forest to a + junction at 12.95km. Go straight over the junction and along a narrow, overhung track which leads downhill to a gate at the edge of a clearing - 13.47km. Go through the gate and wind generally downwards (ignoring a left turn) to another gate at 13.69km. You reach a third gate at 14.12km and GR 772 560, close to a farm building. This gate leads you onto a short tarmac section. Drop to a forest road at 14.35km and GR 773 561. Turn left along the gravel road bearing right at a T-junction at 14.62km. From here, freewheel (mostly) down the winding, wide road, keeping a look out for any forest traffic - there is a depot at the bottom of the hill. At 15.95km, you will pass the depot and must now take extra care as the A5 arrives quickly round a bend at 16.31km and GR 771 575.

Turn left along the A5 to 18.05km. Turn left here and down a narrow road just as the A5 goes over a large stone bridge. Follow this road with views of Moel Siabod to reach Pont Cyfyng at 21km. Turn left, cycling gently up the A5 to reach the end of the ride at 23km.

Views up to Moel Siabod

Route 22 - Circuit of Moel Hebog

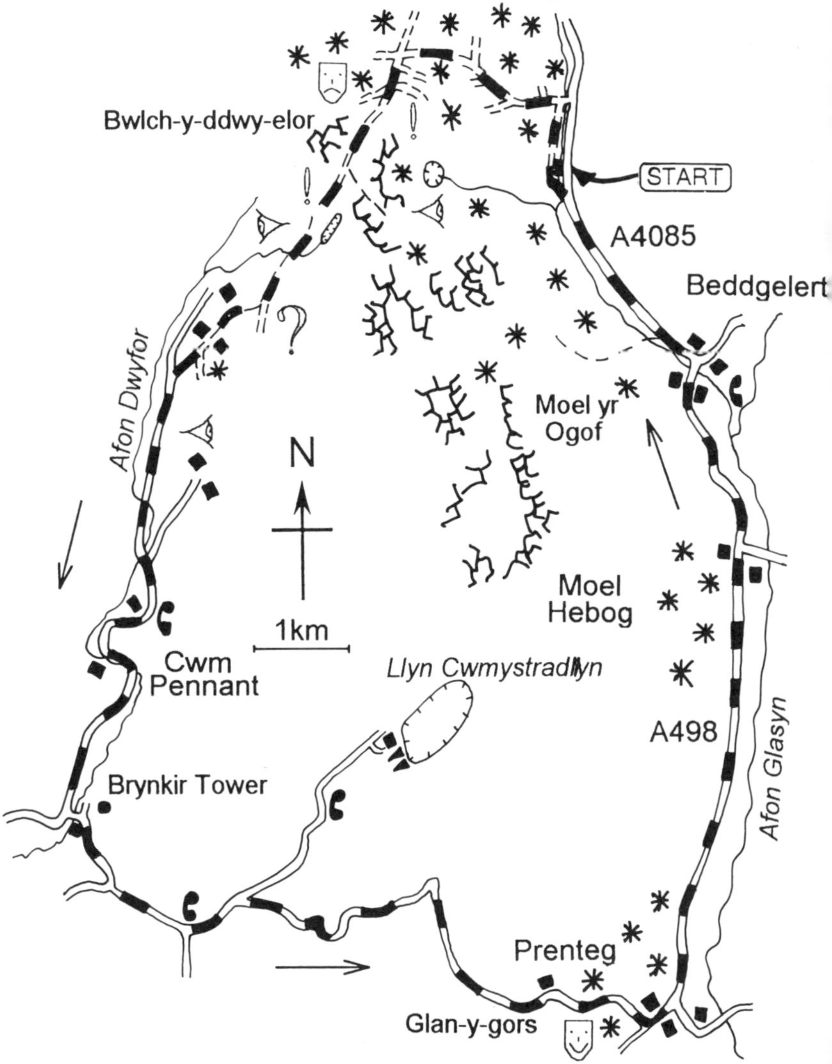

Bwlch-y-ddwy-elor

START

A4085

Beddgelert

Afon Dwyfor

Moel yr
Ogof

N

1km

Moel
Hebog

Cwm
Pennant

Llyn Cwmystradllyn

A498

Brynkir Tower

Afon Glasyn

Prenteg

Glan-y-gors

22. Circuit of Moel Hebog

Glan-yr-gors, Pont Cae'r-gors, Parc Cae-cra, Bwlch-y-ddwy-elor, Cwm Trwsgl, Tyddyn-mawr, Cwm Pennant, Brynkir Tower, Clenenney, Cefn-coch, Llyn Du, Prenteg, Pont Aberglaslyn, Beddgelert, Glan-yr-gors.

Map = OS no. 115 Snowdon, OS No 124 Dolgellau
Best conditions = Any
Length = 35.5km of which 7.5km are off road
Height gain = 600m
Time = 2.5 - 5 hours
Stars = **

This route, though mainly on road, passes through some high mountain scenery and offers an excellent day out. It passes over forest roads, a high col, grassy tracks and wild minor roads. The navigation is straightforward except for one small section well-covered in the text.

Mountain bike races are held twice a year in this forest. At those times a number of the roads will be closed and the organisers ask that you observe any signs and warnings that they erect.

From the Forest Enterprise carpark at Glan yr Gors (GR 573 502) join the forest road which runs parallel to the A4085 and turn left gently uphill. After some 700m you will reach the entrance to the forest where you should turn left and head up into the trees. Follow this steeply up to 1.34km. Take the second right-hand turn just as the road which you have been following begins to descend. Continue for 400m to 1.73km where you go straight on along a narrower track as the other turns sharp left. Follow this new track round, down and up again. At 2.9km you reach a four-way junction with the left-hand track blocked off by five large boulders.

Turn left through the boulders and avoid the missing bridge via a path to the right. Bear left once up the steep bank. Cross the bridge then turn immediately right and head up the hill to a T-junction at 3.23km. Bear right then immediately left following the signs to Dolbenmaen. Climb very steeply up the slaty track as it winds past some old quarries. This section will force the unfit to carry and when wet it will defeat all but the most accomplished rider. You top out at 4.15km at a col called Bwlch-y-ddwy-elor, which offers excellent and different views from each side of the col.

The next section is along a number of bridleways that will be subject to changes and rebuilding over the next few years. If you are in any doubt as to which way to go, you should follow the new signposts which I am told will be in place soon. In particular the RUPP which leads to Brithdir Mawr farm will be downgraded to bridleway and opened up, whilst the bridleway leading to Blaen Pennant will be downgraded to footpath status.

Drop down the far side passing a gate at 4.25km. Bear left down a rough track through marsh grass. Descend for 200m then keep to the left side of the slope and descend steep and difficult terrain heading for the obvious lake below.

Note: Do not drop down the incline to the right as there are several missing bridges! Cycle pleasantly above the lake (GR 548 496) then drop down close to the next incline to reach a recently rebuilt bridge at 5.2km. Cross the bridge and follow the muddy track for 700m until you are above a small plantation. Drop to the nearest end of this, then pass along its upper edge to reach its southern end and a gate at 6km. Go through the gate then directly over the small plateau in front towards some small trees where you will pick up the top of a vague track at 6.07km. Zigzag down this track then head over towards an old barn some distance away. At 6.5km you go through a narrow gate just beyond a stream then follow the fence/wall towards the barn. Do not go through a large black gate but continue over to the barn which you reach at 6.75km.

Go past the barn on a good track watching out for some fencing stretched over the track (a surrogate gate). Drop to a country lane which you reach at a bridge at 7.35km.

Turn left and follow the narrow road down the lovely Cwm Pennant bearing right at a chapel and telephone box to 13km. Turn left over a bridge in front of a white house. Follow the road to the right in front of a wooded hill with a tower (Twr Brynkir) on it. Turn left at a T-junction at 14.3km just after a short, steep hill. At 15.35km follow a signpost to Cwm Ystradlyn by turning left. Then at 16.65km turn right towards Tremadog through a gate on a hillside.

You may wish to continue along this road to the beautiful Llyn Ystradlyn and an interesting old slate mill on the way, before returning and taking the Tremadog road.

Follow the road over the moors then downhill past the caravan park at 25km before reaching the A498 at a T-junction at 25.7km. Turn left following this road to Beddgelert where you bear left over the bridge and climb out of the village. At 34.2km turn second left down a narrow lane past some houses and into the forest to reach the carpark at 35.3km.

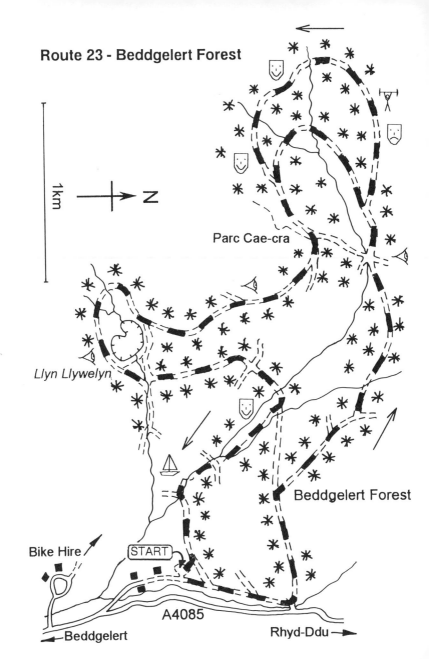

Route 23 - Beddgelert Forest

1km

N

Parc Cae-cra

Llyn Llywelyn

Beddgelert Forest

Bike Hire

START

A4085

← Beddgelert

Rhyd-Ddu →

23. Beddgelert Forest

Glan y Gors, Pont Cae'r-gors, Moelfryn, Cwm Du, Parc Cae-cra, Llyn Llywelyn, Parc Tanciau, Parc Cae-mawr, Glan y Gors.

Map = OS no. 115 Snowdon or Outdoor Leisure 17 Snowdonia
Best conditions = Any
Length = 10km, entirely off road
Height gain = 270m
Time = 1 hour plus
Stars = *

This route starts from Glan y Gors forest carpark at GR 573 502. It utilises forest roads and tracks and is a short but interesting introduction to Beddgelert Forest. Bike hire is available from Beddgelert Bikes, Hafod Ruffydd Uchaf (076686) 434, GR 569 495. NB! A bike computer is practically an essential for this route.

Mountain bike races are held twice a year in this forest. At those times a number of the roads will be closed and the organisers ask that you observe any signs and warnings that they erect.

From the forest carpark at GR 573 502 head onto the forest road which runs parallel to the main A4085. Turn left and follow it uphill for 700m as far as its junction with the main road. Turn left climbing into the trees to 1.35km where you take the second right. Follow this bearing left at 1.75km. Drop then climb steadily until you cross a small bridge at 2.8km and GR 557 512.

Just after the bridge turn right. Drop down the bank and follow the path to the next track. Turn left at 2.86km then fork right just beyond.

At 3.02km turn right up the grassy track which climbs very steeply up into a higher part of the forest. Follow this with some difficulty (100m or so of carry and several fallen trees to pass) until you reach some fallen trees just after a small stream.

Carry up the right bank to reach another track 15m beyond at 3.92km. Turn left dropping quickly down the hillside to 5.25km. Here you join another track and continue in the same direction passing a left turn at 5.46km and GR 556 509.

Follow the main track round to the right at a fork at 5.56km then fork left at 6.06km and GR 559 506. Drop to 6.7km (GR 560 500) where you bear right and follow the track up and round the back of Llyn Llywelyn.

At 7.63km cut left along the edge of the lake with some fine views. You then cross a narrow bridge before turning right at the far side of the lake at 7.83km. Drop to a + junction at 7.93km and GR 563 500 where you turn left. Go straight over the next + junction at 8.59km then turn right down a single track at 8.84km, GR 564 508.

At this point you should take extra care to avoid excessive speed due to the presence of walkers on the track.

At 9.35km go straight over the next track and continue down the narrow path to a stream at 9.41km. Cross the stream then bump down the rough track beyond to 9.65km. Turn left here and follow this track until it is possible to drop to the carpark at 10.2km.

Llyn Llywelyn. Photo C. Bursnall

Route 24 - Bwlch Cwm Llan

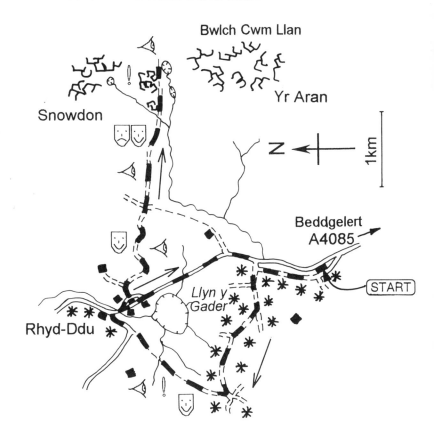

24. Bwlch Cwm Llan

Glan yr Gors, Cwm Marchnad, Drwsycoed Uchaf, Rhyd-Ddu, Pen ar Lon, Bwlch Cwm Llan, Pen ar Lon, Rhyd-Ddu, Pont Cae'r-gors, Glan yr Gors.

Map = OS no. 115 Snowdon
Best Conditions = Early or late to avoid walkers
Length = 16km of which 3km are on road
Height gain = 450m
Time = 1.5 - 3 hours
Stars = ***

This beautiful and surprisingly gentle route starts from Glan yr Gors forest carpark at GR 573 502. Though short in length, it passes through some lovely scenery and offers some of the best views in the area. The riding is very straightforward except for perhaps 200m where you may have to carry. Ideally suited to those with children or those who do not want a high speed thrash and will appreciate their surroundings.
Note: this route is covered by the voluntary ban between the 1st of June to the 30th of September. This means that you should avoid it between the hours of 10 a.m. and 5 p.m. during this period.

From the forest carpark at GR 573 502 join the forest road which runs parallel to the A4085. Turn left climbing gently to the entrance to the forest at 7km. Turn left here and climb into the forest proper. At 1.34km take the second right turn just as the road in front of you begins to drop. Follow this to 1.73km where you go straight on as the main track bears left and down. This track leads you down and then up again to 2.9km. You will reach a + junction with the left turn blocked by five large boulders at GR 557 512.

Turn right climbing out of the forest to gain good views as you pass through a wall at 3.1km. You will then drop through a gate and ford a small stream at 3.46km. Descend roughly through Cwm Marchnad to two gates at 3.93km. Go through the first one and then follow the white-painted arrows across the field beyond. These will lead you down towards Drwsycoed Uchaf farm and to some gateposts at 4.36km. Continue down to the next gate but bear right in front of it along an extremely rough track. This leads you round the edge of the field below the farm and up to a gate at 4.77km.

Go through the gate and follow the road down to a T-junction with the A4085 in the village of Rhyd-Ddu at 5.25km. Turn right and climb gently through the village. At 5.47km you turn left following a footpath sign between houses to reach a metal five-bar gate and a kissing gate at 5.64km.

Note: the next 1.5km are along one of the main paths to Snowdon so please have consideration for walkers.

Go through the gate and ride up the stony track beyond. Just before the first gate at 6km you will pass a very small quarry which has been bolted for climbing! Someone, somewhere is desperate for a piece of the action!

Continue up through a second gate/stile at 7.11km, which leads you to Pen ar Lon (good views of the Nantlle ridge). Here the path to Snowdon bears off to the left. Ignore this small turning and continue on the track passing through a third and final gate at 7.25km.

The good quarry track now leads you above a boggy area and up towards Yr Aran - a much underrated and rarely visited mountain which has breathtaking views from its summit. The track slowly steepens and at 8.7km, after a short, tricky climb, you reach the first of the quarry workings. The views back from this point are very good and it is a good spot to sit and take in the atmosphere.

The next section contains all the difficulty, so keep to the main left-hand track and climb steeply up through the workings with some difficulty (not insurmountable for the skilled). Eventually you reach a level section with two stiles on the right, a quarry hole on the left and an incline to the front at 9.26km.

Climb the incline and through the remains of the drum room at the top. Head along the slate track beyond until it turns to grass. The grassy path will then lead you to the wall at Bwlch Cwm Llan at 9.65km. Park the bikes and step through the wall to marvel at the view beyond over the Moelwyns, Moel Siabod, Lliwedd and - if you drop down the slope for a few metres - Snowdon.

The return trip is straightforward except for the incline which is fun for the mad or a carry for the rest.

Note: at 11.7km you will join the Snowdon path and the walkers on it so slow down and give way to them. It is only for 1.5km so please be responsible.

At 13.21km you will reach the locked gate and kissing gate. Go through it then turn left. Head out through the carpark and out onto the A4085 where you turn left. Follow the road back to the entrance to the forest at Pont Cae'r-gors at 15.25km. Go into the forest and drop down the track parallel to the road to return to the carpark at 16km. Now go and get that film developed!

Route 25 - Maesgwm (Telegraph Valley)

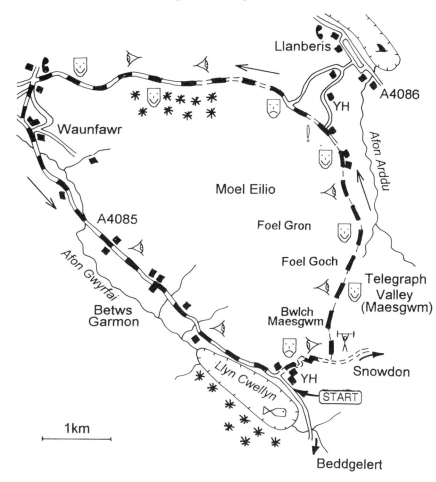

25. Maesgwm (Telegraph Valley)

Snowdon Ranger carpark, Bwlch Maesgwm, Maesgwm, Brithdir, Maen-llwyd-isaf, Donen Las, Waunfawr, Betws Garmon, Snowdon Ranger carpark.

Map = OS no. 115 Snowdon or Outdoor Leisure 17 Snowdonia
Best conditions = Early or late to avoid trekkers
Length = 19km of which 10km are on minor roads
Height gain = 500m
Time = 1.5-3 hours
Stars = ***

This route starts from the Snowdon Ranger carpark at GR 564 550. It uses narrow tracks, unclassified minor roads and minor roads to give one of the most enjoyable routes in the area. Better than slogging to the summit of the sacrificial mountain, this route is a pleasure to ride. It is best done first thing in the morning or last thing in the evening when there are fewer walkers on the zigzags which provide one of the main routes up Snowdon.

From the Snowdon Ranger carpark at GR 564 550 go onto the road and straight over it bearing slightly right and following the signposts which lead you behind a house and onto a track. Turn right, up the track and pass behind the last house at 280m. Follow the path up through a gate and then work steadily up the zigzags which are almost entirely rideable. However, if you find your wheels spinning, either let some air out of your tires to get more traction or get off and walk - either way, avoid further erosion of the path.

At the top of the zigzags you will go through a wall at 1.19km (though you may have gone through a different, more painful wall by now!).

Continue up a steep section which you may have to walk. At 1.46km you reach a small wooden waymarking post which points to Llanberis.

Turn left and carry up the steep, grassy hillside more or less along the line of the telegraph pole stumps for 250m. The angle eases at some very small rock outcrops (from here there are excellent views of the Nantlle Ridge and Moel Hebog).

Pedal up the grassy path to a fence and stile at 1.86km. Pass over this and continue on to a wall and stile at a col, 2.08km. From the far side of Bwlch Maesgwm there is an interesting view down to Llanberis and the Dinorwig quarries which you may not have seen before.

Note: this section of bridleway is frequently used by pony trekking groups during the summer months. Mountain bikers must give way to horse-riders. The thought of frightened horses bolting in this situation conjures up nightmare scenarios for the future of mountain biking in Snowdonia.

Drop down the excellent track beyond which can be completely iced over during cold weather - as I discovered to my cost when I suddenly found myself skating down a 30m patch of ice with nothing but a steep drop on the right to comfort me!

Follow the track down until at Brithdir it becomes metalled (5.2km). Continue along the road until you reach the far end of a straight section, near a house at 5.75km. Go straight on through a gate where the road bends down to the right and pass along the excellent, rough track. This takes you to another metalled track at 6.47km just below Maes-llwyd-isaf.

Turn left and climb steeply up the hill and onto a stony track where the metal ends. Keep climbing until the track levels out but do not forget to look back as the views are beautiful from here. At 7.82km you will reach a gate that overlooks the Domen Las plantation. Drop to the trees and join the head of a minor road at 8.5km. Fly down this road until the views of Moel Hebog, Nantlle Ridge, the Rivals and Anglesey force you to stop and admire them.

Zoooom down to a + junction above Waunfawr at 11.05km. Turn left and left again at 11.34km. This road will bring you out at a junction with the A4085 at 12.4km. Turn left and cycle through Betws Garmon and beside Llyn Cwellyn until you return to the carpark at 19km.

Descending the narrow trail towards Llanberis
with Elidir Fawr in the background

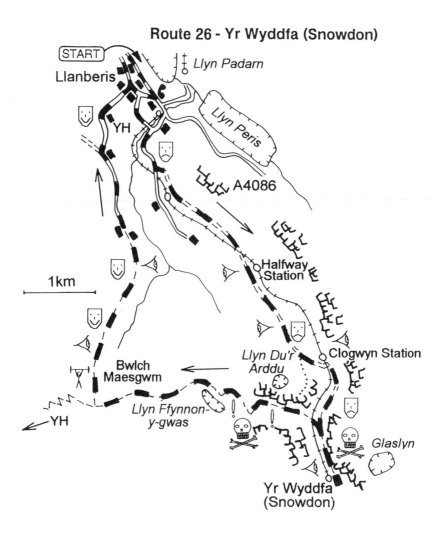

Route 26 - Yr Wyddfa (Snowdon)

START

Llanberis

Llyn Padarn

Llyn Peris

A4086

YH

1km

Halfway Station

Clogwyn Station

Bwlch Maesgwm

Llyn Du'r Arddu

Llyn Ffynnon-y-gwas

Glaslyn

YH

Yr Wyddfa (Snowdon)

26. Yr Wyddfa (Snowdon)

Llanberis, Halfway House, Clogwyn Station, Garnedd Ugain, Yr Wyddfa, Clogwyn Du'r Arddu, Llyn Ffynnon-y-gwas, Bwlch Maesgwm, Tynyraelgerth, Llanberis.

Map = OS no. 115 Snowdon
Best Conditions = Early or late to avoid walkers
Length = 20km of which 5km are on minor roads
Height gain = 1100m
Time = 2.5-5 hours
Stars = **

This hard route uses several of the Snowdon bridleways to produce a mountain bikers' horseshoe and aims to lessen the impact of cyclists on other mountain users by avoiding the excessive speed displayed by some people on the Llanberis path. It is not an easy route and if you are not fit then you should try a less strenuous route which you will enjoy more! However, Snowdon is of vital importance to mountain bikers being the only 3000ft mountain that is legally rideable in the country. It is also a source of much controversy, so if you do ride it then be on your best behaviour or we will be thrown off it.

This route is subject to voluntary restrictions agreed by the National Park and cycling bodies which asks mountain bikers to avoid the mountain and its bridleways between the hours of 10 a.m. and 5 p.m. from the 1st of June until the 30th of September. This ban pertains to all bridleways leading to the summit of Snowdon but not those leading through Maesgwm (Telegraph Valley).

From the lakeside carpark at GR 577 604 opposite Pete's Eats (you know the one!) head along the A4086 then turn right into the village after 0.62km Take the next left turn just after the BP garage at 0.82km along a road that leads you back under the Snowdon railway and to a T-junction at 1.6km. Turn right and get into a sensible gear for the start of the long climb to the summit.

This very steep hill leads you up next to Coed Victoria and past some houses. At 2.55km the Llanberis path bears off to the left just before the brow of a hill. Go through the gate past the "No motorbikes or cars" sign and along the rough track.

The first section of path has some rocky steps on it which you will probably have to carry over. It is mostly rideable until you reach a gate at 3.29km. Beyond the gate the going eases until you carry over a short rocky step at 4.34km and then at 4.48km pass under the railway line and ride a tricky rock step just beyond.

Continue gently to 5.41km when you reach the halfway house (the building was blown down at the time of printing this book). From here you can admire the view of Clogwyn Du'r Arddu, Moel Eilio and, if you can work it out, the route back through Maesgwm.

Keep on the track to 6.31km where there is a fork beside a new fence and a small cairn. The right-hand track goes to Cloggy but you should take the left option as it climbs steeply up to Clogwyn Station. How much of this you ride depends on how fit you are and how good your bike is. You reach the station at 7km having carried some of the way. Pass under the railway line enjoying a brief respite from the pain and some great views down into Llanberis pass and over the Glyders.

Climb to the left of the railway for 150m until you come briefly alongside it near a danger sign. Bear left up the very steep bridleway and test your fitness and resolve once again!

Note: do not follow the railway as this is not a right of way and accidents with trains have occurred.

Somewhere on Garnedd Ugain the track will level off sufficiently to allow you to get back on your bike. Pass the standing stone at Bwlch Glas (the top of the Pyg Track zigzags) at 8.5km and follow the rough track close to the left of the railway. Keep away from the

Snowdon and Clogwyn Du'r Arddu under light spring snow

cliff edge until you reach the summit at 9.2km. Well done! By the way, if our cycle computers do not tally it is because of the carrying

It is important to park your bike sensibly at the summit as there have been incidents of elderly people (who come up by train) tripping over badly placed bikes. Also, please do not take bikes into the café building!

Note: on the way down you must restrict your speed and give way to walkers as accidents have happened.

Once you have recovered enough to think of descending, retrace your steps carefully to the Pyg Track standing stone. A little beyond it on the other side of the railway is a similar though smaller stone at the top of the Snowdon Ranger path. Cross to this at 10km and follow the path roughly down towards the top of Clogwyn Du'r Arddu. Then head down the zigzags which will require some carrying, again depending on how technically able you are - 1km is not unreasonable.

You will reach the bottom of the zigzags at 12km above Llyn Ffynnon-y-gwas. You can then cycle along the easy path beyond until you reach a gate at 12.6km. Continue along the now boggy track to reach another gate at 13.7km. Remember to carry over the bogs to minimise your impact.

At 13.96km you reach a small post with "path to Llanberis" on it at the bottom of a slope with the remains of some telegraph poles strewn about. Turn right and carry up the slope next to the telegraph stumps for 250m until the angle eases and you can cycle up the grassy path. Go through two gates/stile to reach Bwlch Maesgwm at 14.6km with its excellent views towards Llanberis.

Note: please watch out for pony trekkers if you do this route in the summer as a horse bolting on the steep hillside could be fatal for it and the rider.

Drop down the great path through Maesgwm doing the Telegraph Valley boogy, through a gate and past some houses, trying not to land in the first one because of too much speed.

Follow the track as it becomes a road and crosses a stream before bearing sharp right at 18.25km. Follow the road steeply down past Llanberis YHA until you reach a T-junction in Llanberis at 19.7km. Turn left here then right in front of and past Pete's Eats (if you can bear to ride past!) to reach the carpark at 20.1km. Lock up the bikes then make a bolt for Pete's Eats to beat the queue and refill your fuel tank!

Early morning view of Dolbadarn Castle at the foot
of the Snowdon route.

OTHER RIDES

There are a number of other rides in the area not covered in this
guide. Most of these are within the four forest areas. These are
waymarked routes of all levels and information on them is available
from the forest Visitor Centres.

There are also a number of short bridleway sections from which
you can devise your own routes, and some pleasant minor roads on
the Lleyn Peninsular.

There is a cycle route from Caernarfon to Porthmadog following
an old railway line and this is marked on the 1:50 000 scale maps.

Further south in Mid Wales there are a wealth of remote bridleways
and minor roads just waiting for you to pick up the map!

The Lake District, The Howgills & The Yorkshire Dales

JEREMY ASHCROFT

36 selected routes amongst England's finest mountains; some completely new, some established classics.

All levels of ability catered for - routes across summits, passes, moorland, & along valleys.

Each route lavishly illustrated with freshly drawn maps in 2 colours, and b&w photos depicting the variety of terrain and weather conditions.

Clearly written route descriptions. Guidance on equipment, mountain survival and access & conservation.

ISBN 0 948153-10-5 **£7.50**

Breaking Loose

DAVE COOK

'The mass of men lead live of quiet desperation', and few realise their dreams of escape. Dave Cook followed his dream and in 1989 set off for Australia on his bicycle. His vivid account tells of rock-climbing adventures en route, of friends made and of the political situations he found - including a tangle with Saddam Hussein's police. Throughout he records with keen observation and refreshing honesty his reflections on social injustice from Yugoslavia to the Indian continent; and on his own moral values and the pursuit of dreams.

ISBN 0 948153-26-1 **£9.50**

To order by mail, send a cheque made out to THE ERNEST PRESS adding 10% for post & packing.
THE ERNEST PRESS, 1 THOMAS STREET, HOLYHEAD LL65 1RR.

More routes in The Lakes, Howgills & The Yorkshire Dales

JEREMY ASHCROFT

Due to the great demand from the author's first Mountain Bike Guide to the Lakes, Howgills and Yorkshire Dales, this second book has been compiled. Using the same format with superb two-colour maps and clear route descriptions, this second group of 36 routes provides the same variety of challenge, from family rides to full-blown mountain adventures.

ISBN 0 948153-13-X   **£7.50**

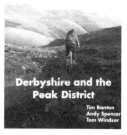

Derbyshire and the Peak District

TIM BANTON, ANDY SPENCER, TOM WINDSOR

Pick a ride, pack your butties and pedal. Choose from 21 easily accessible legal routes. Varying between 7 and 40 miles, each circular route has clear instructions, a sketch map and illustrations. These rides, compiled by 3 local authors, use tracks and bridleways through contrasting but adjacent landscapes. They explore an area where upland and lowland Britain meet. Whether you prefer high gritstone moors, limestone dales or wooded parkland, one taste and you will be back for more!

ISBN 0 948153-12-1   **£6.95**

Northumberland

DEREK PURDY

32 well researched, totally legal routes throughout Northumberland, the best kept mountain biking secret in England. Bridleways, forest tracks, old drove-roads, ancient commercial routes, and neglected country roads.
Each route beautifully illustrated with black and white photos, two-colour maps, accompanied by technical terrain analysis and plotting plan, clearly written route descriptions including a little local history and colour.
There are routes for all abilities.

ISBN 0 948153-16-4   **£7.50**

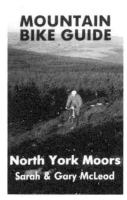

North York Moors

SARAH & GARY McLEOD

20 well-researched and legal routes over the open space of
the North York Moors. Careful attention to conservation per-
meates the text with sites of potential erosion highlighted.
All routes are clearly described and illustrated with two-
colour maps and numerous photographs.
The guide caters well for family days but points out longer
days through route linking for the young and fit.

ISBN 0 948153-30-X

£6.95

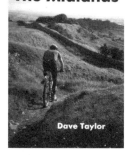

The Midlands

DAVE TAYLOR

This is the Mountain Bike Guide - family edition. The pages
are packed with routes for fun days out or peaceful summer
evenings in beautiful countryside.
But, Hammerheads, do not dismay! There are plenty of pun-
ishing climbs and the potential for some long, challenging
days out.
Each of the 21 routes is illustrated with black and white photos and includes a two-colour sketch-map, local history etc.

ISBN 0 948153-29-6

£6.95

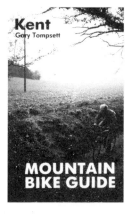

Kent

GARY TOMPSETT

21 well-researched circular routes throughout Kent - the garden
of England. Discover this intricate county using the carefully
drawn sketch-maps and clearly written route descriptions. Each
route is accompanied by an unusual wealth of information on
local history and geography, attractions and off route amenities
and access rights. Black and white illustrations show the rich
variety of landscapes visited. There are routes for all abilities,
between 5 and 50 km, providing an essential guide for all off
road cyclists. Beginners, families and expert riders will delight in
the variety on offer. Just jump on your bike and go.

ISBN 0 94815-34-2

£6.95